07 JULY 2016

Dear Pamela,

Thank you for your ongoing
friendship and contact over the
past years.

We wish health and mobility for you.

I hope this book will provide you
with some joy and insight
into South Africa

It was delightful to see you again.

much love,

MARTIN, ANNEKE, ADAM, JULIET & ZAC.

Contents

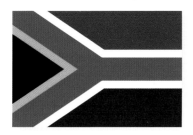

SOUTH AFRICA at a glance

- **Official name:** Republic of South Africa
- **National motto:** *!ke e:/xarra//ke (diverse people unite)*
- **Size:** 1 219 090 km²
- **Currency:** Rand (ZAR) [100 cents equals one rand]
- **Capitals:** Pretoria (administrative), Cape Town (legislative), Bloemfontein (judicial)
- **Type of government:** Constitutional democracy in a three-tier system (local, provincial, national)
- **Number of provinces:** 9 - Eastern Cape, Free State, Gauteng, KwaZulu-Natal , Limpopo, Mpumalanga, North West , Northern Cape, Western Cape,
- **Population:** 52 982 000
- **Languages:** 11 official languages – Afrikaans, English, isiNdebele , isiXhosa , isiZulu , Sesotho , Sesotho sa Leboa , Setswana, siSwati, Tshivenda, Xitsonga
- **Date of first democratic election:** 27 April 1994 (27 April is celebrated annually as 'Freedom Day' and is a public holiday)
- **Longest River:** Orange River
- **Highest mountain peak:** Mafadi (Drakensberg) 3, 450m
- **Largest desert:** Kalahari Desert
- **Neighbouring countries:** Lesotho, Swaziland, Mozambique, Zimbabwe, Botswana, Namibia
- **Bordering Oceans:** Atlantic on the west coast, Indian on the East Coast
- **National bird:** blue crane (*Anthropoides paradisia*)
- **National fish:** galjoen (*Dichistius capensis*)
- **National animal:** springbok (*Antidorcas marsupialis*)
- **National flower:** king protea (*Protea cynaroides*)
- **National tree:** real yellowwood (*Podocarpus latifolius*)
- **Time:** GMT +2 hours

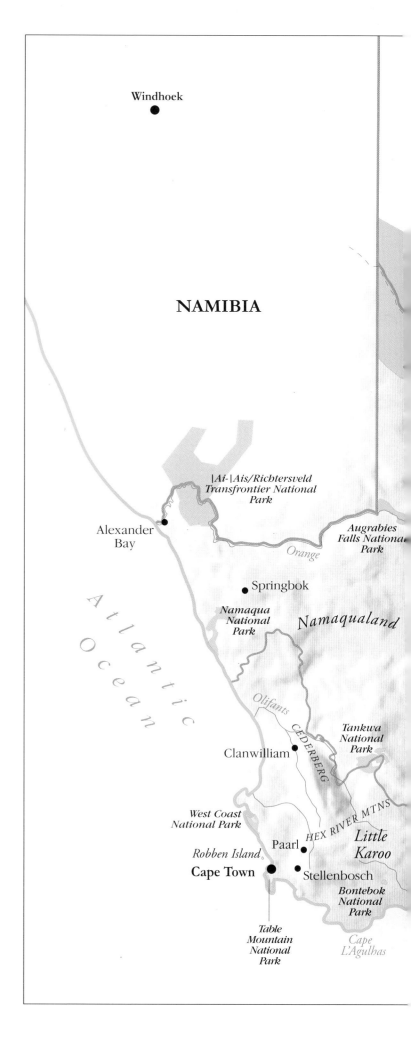

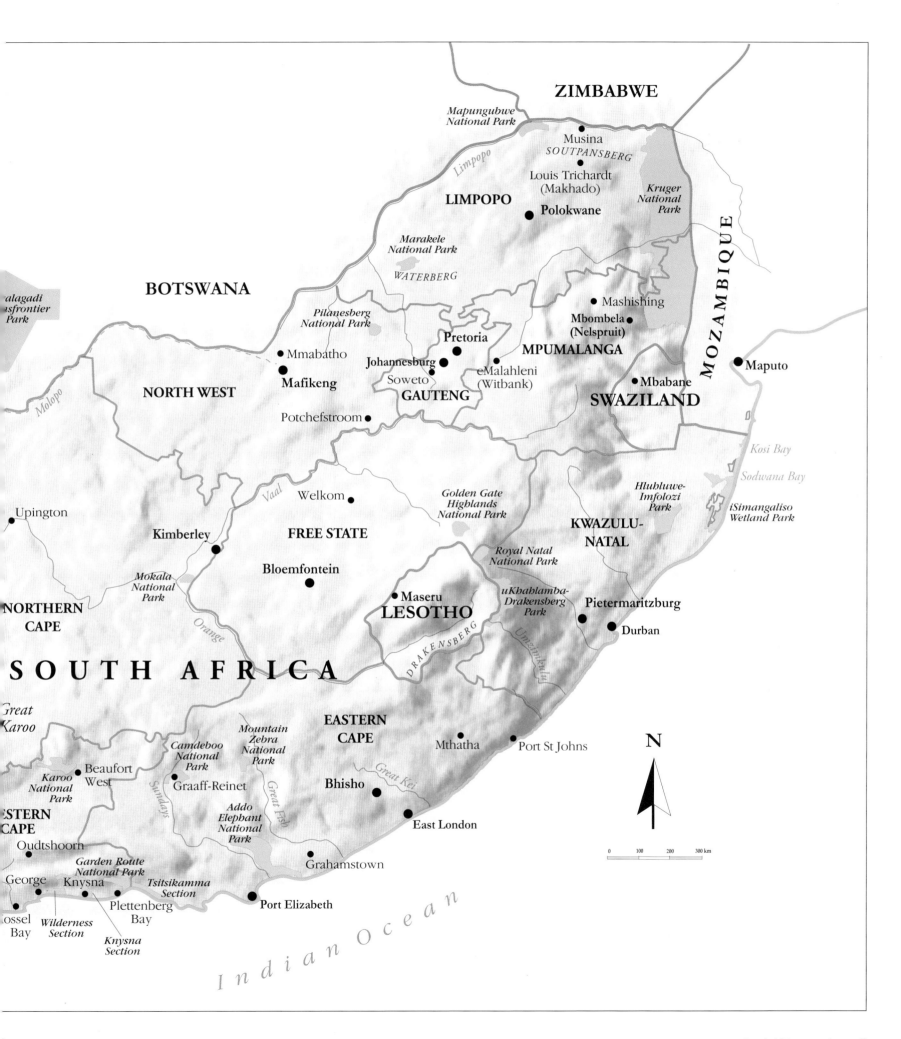

ZIMBABWE

Mapungubwe National Park

Musina
SOUTPANSBERG

Louis Trichardt (Makhado)

LIMPOPO

Kruger National Park

Polokwane

BOTSWANA

Marakele National Park

WATERBERG

MOZAMBIQUE

Mashishing

Pilanesberg National Park

Mbombela (Nelspruit)

Pretoria

Mmabatho

MPUMALANGA

Maputo

Johannesburg

Mafikeng

Soweto
eMalahleni (Witbank)

Mbabane

NORTH WEST

GAUTENG

SWAZILAND

Potchefstroom

Kosi Bay

Molopo

Vaal

Welkom

Golden Gate Highlands National Park

Sodwana Bay

Hluhluwe-Imfolozi Park

Upington

iSimangaliso Wetland Park

Kimberley

FREE STATE

KWAZULU-NATAL

Royal Natal National Park

Mokala National Park

Bloemfontein

Orange

Maseru

uKhahlamba-Drakensberg Park

Pietermaritzburg

NORTHERN CAPE

LESOTHO

DRAKENSBERG

Durban

Umzimkulu

S O U T H   A F R I C A

Great Karoo

Mountain Zebra National Park

EASTERN CAPE

Mthatha

Port St Johns

N

Camdeboo National Park

Great Kei

Karoo National Park

Beaufort West

Graaff-Reinet

Bhisho

0   100   200   300 km

ESTERN CAPE

Addo Elephant National Park

Great Fish

Sundays

East London

Oudtshoorn

Garden Route National Park

George

Knysna

Tsitsikamma Section

Grahamstown

ossel Bay

Wilderness Section

Plettenberg Bay

Knysna Section

Port Elizabeth

I n d i a n   O c e a n

The De Hoop Nature Reserve in the Western Cape.

South Africa: a world in one country

The Republic of South Africa is a large country by any standard, and a varied one too. Its 1 220 430 km² cover high central plateau and game-rich bushveld, forested upland, dry semi-desert and fertile coastal terrace that, together, embrace a rich diversity of ethnic groups, cultures, creeds and languages.

And it is diversity which best describes this country of hope and unity, a country that has shown the world how adversity can be overcome and how different peoples can be united by a common goal and the right to be free. But this human diversity is also the product of a turbulent and often tragic history that goes back millennia, to the Stone Age hunter-gatherers of the sunlit plains and the Bantu-speaking migrants who came from the north to supplant them. In modern times, the story has been one of European conquest and colonisation and, latterly, of an oppressed people's increasingly effective resistance to a monumentally unjust political system.

Today, after more than a decade of democracy, South Africa is at peace with itself, free to chart its course, and confident of its future. It is also a country whose scenic beauty and infinite variety captivates both its own people and those who come here to explore what it has to offer.

▶ South Africa is known worldwide as 'The Rainbow Nation', a true testament to its diversity of peoples, cultures and natural landscapes.

'…working together, we can and shall succeed in meeting the common objective we have set ourselves as a nation – to build a better life for all …' former president Thabo Mbeki, 2007

Pointers to the past

The San, hunter-gatherers whose vivid artistry adorns thousands of rocky sites from the Drakensberg mountains in the east to the Atlantic coast in the west, were among the first people to inhabit South Africa. Next came the pastoralist Khoekhoen who, for the most part, settled the western, west-central and southern regions of the subcontinent. Later came the Bantu-speaking agropastoralists, who began to filter southwards across the Limpopo River around 200 CE in a slow migration that gathered momentum over the centuries. By the mid-1600s the Sotho, Tsonga and others had spread across much of the interior plateau, and the Nguni had moved down and along the Indian Ocean seaboard, the Xhosa or southern Nguni becoming entrenched in what is now the Eastern Cape.

Although Bartolomeu Dias rounded the Cape of Good Hope in 1488 on his way to establishing a sea route to India, and Portuguese seafarers regularly made stops along the South African coast, European settlement only took place from 1652 onwards when Jan van Riebeeck was instructed by the Dutch East India Company to establish a station at Table Bay to provide provisions to passing ships.

Within a few years, European settlers were granted farms in the area and the seeds of a colony were sown, to be nurtured in 1688 by the arrival of French Huguenots fleeing religious persecution in France. But while the settlement continued to grow, the Dutch East India Company became overextended and corrupt, which eventually led to occupation by the British in 1806 and the establishment of the Cape of Good Hope as a British colony a few years later. As many white settlers moved further from the seat of government in Cape Town, so the frontiers of the colony were adjusted. As the border was progressively shifted eastward, more land became the property of the British Crown, to be sold or 'loaned' to settlers even though, in many instances, it was already occupied and used by the Xhosa and other indigenous peoples. In 1820, the first of thousands of British immigrants were placed on allotments along the eastern frontier, partly in the hope that their numbers alone would help to quell resistance by the resident Xhosa. Conflict over territorial rights was inevitable and several 'frontier wars' were fought.

Around the same time a new power had appeared in KwaZulu-Natal – the militaristic and expansionist kingdom of the Zulu under Shaka. Although he had allowed a handful of British to settle at Port Natal (now Durban), if Shaka had still been alive in the late 1830s he would undoubtedly have opposed large-scale settlement by Cape Dutch, or Boer, families, known as Voortrekkers. They had left the Cape soon after the emancipation of slaves, in a movement that came to be known as the Great Trek.

After the British annexed Natal, the Voortrekkers loaded up their wagons again, this time to join their compatriots on the Highveld, in the process defeating and dispossessing the indigenous peoples who opposed them. The Boers eventually did manage to establish their own independent republics – the Transvaal (later the South African Republic) in 1852, and the Orange Free State two years later.

▶ Various rock art sites, such as this one at Salmanslaagte in the Cederberg, are scattered across the South African landscape, evidence of the artistry of the San hunter-gatherers who lived here thousands of years ago.

The discovery of gold on the Witwatersrand in 1886 led to serious tension between Britain and the republics and eventually to the Anglo-Boer (South African) War of 1899–1902. After the Boers were defeated, the republics were united with the Cape of Good Hope and Natal in the Union of South Africa, which was granted self-governing status. However, the hardline Afrikaner was determined to regain his lost independence, while blacks had almost no say in national affairs.

In 1912 the South African Native National Congress was founded, which was to become the African National Congress (ANC), a black organisation dedicated, in its early years, to peaceful opposition to an unjust system. The next year, 1913, saw an act of parliament that created 'white' areas and 'black' areas throughout the country, the framework for future development along apartheid lines.

Subsequent years saw more discrimatory laws put in place by successive Union governments, designed to exclude the African people entirely from the political, social and economic mainstream. In 1948 the National Party came into power and, over the next 40 years of its rule, apartheid – 'apartness' or 'separateness' – was introduced into almost every sphere of private and public life.

The overall policy was to create 'homelands', where all black people could be allocated to a particular area which, in time, would be granted 'independence' by South Africa. This policy was rigorously enforced, and particular examples include Sophiatown in Johannesburg and District Six in Cape Town, where tens of thousands of people were forcibly removed from their homes, loaded onto trucks and resettled in undeveloped outlying areas.

Despite the growing burdens of apartheid, South Africa appeared to prosper, even after withdrawing from the British Commonwealth as an independent republic in 1961. But appearances were deceptive. Opposition to apartheid was growing, both locally and internationally. The shooting of blacks by police at Sharpeville in 1960, during a campaign against the pass laws, provoked critical world attention. More violence by police against pupils protesting against the apartheid education system on 16 June 1976 was met by outrage from the international community.

South Africa withdrew even further into isolation. Over the next decade or so the liberation movement put increasing pressure on the government until finally, in February 1990, President FW de Klerk announced a reform package that would lead to full democracy. Long-banned organisations were legalised and a mass of apartheid legislation was scrapped. In particular, the world's imagination was captured by the release of Nelson Mandela from prison after 27 years.

After several gruelling negotiations over a four-year period – a time of sustained mass action, political violence and, occasionally, of assassination – South Africans of all races went to the polls at the end of April 1994 to cast their votes. Ten days later Nelson Mandela became the first president of a democratic South Africa.

After more than a decade of democracy, South Africa has made great strides in implementing equality and improving the lives of all its citizens. While there may still be a long way to go, the country and its people have made it clear to the world that they are dedicated to a better life for all.

▶ The reality of the apartheid years (above left). ▶ As part of the Constitution Hill Project, the once-notorious Old Fort Prison complex (above right) in Johannesburg now houses the Constitutional Court. ▶ Nelson Rolihlahla Mandela (opposite), the first president of a democratic South Africa.

These are the people

South Africa is home to more than 48 million people and the population is made up of the following groups: the Nguni (Zulu, Xhosa, Ndebele and Swazi); Sotho-Tswana (including Southern, Western and Northern Sotho); Tsonga; Venda; Afrikaners; English; coloureds; Indians; and those who have immigrated here from Europe, Asia and the rest of Africa.

This diversity of cultures and peoples is also reflected in the country's 11 official languages, the various religions practised and observed, including Christianity, Islam, Hinduism, Buddhism and Judaism, and the traditional heritage that makes South Africa such a multi-cultural society.

The make-up of South Africa's population is also a clear reflection of the country's history. While the Khoekhoen no longer survive as a distinct race and only a few San still live within the country's borders, it is the Nguni who make up the majority of South Africa's people. The Western Cape is the part of South Africa longest settled by Europeans, and the region to which came the first of the many and varied peoples whose descendants make up the modern Cape's multi-cultural social fabric. Few of these ancestors came voluntarily; most were slaves from Angola, Madagascar, India and the East Indian islands.

KwaZulu-Natal's Indian community is largely descended from the indentured labourers who came to work on the sugar plantations from about the middle of the nineteenth century. Afrikaners are descended from the Dutch, as well as the French Huguenots, and there are also many descendants of the British and Portuguese still living in South Africa.

▶ South Africa is a multi-cultural society, and its people are as diverse as its cultures, religions and language groups.

Sporting South Africa

In South Africa, sport is a religion. No matter what their culture, race group or language, when it comes to competing internationally South Africans all worship at the same altar. But it wasn't always so …

As South Africa was a former colony, its major sports had their roots in British sporting traditions. Rugby and cricket were introduced in the early colonial days and remain two of the favourite spectator sports to this day.

Before and during the apartheid years, rugby and cricket were certainly the monopoly of white South Africa, while football (known locally as soccer) became the sport of choice among black South Africans in the townships. Although most sports funding went towards the white schools and areas, lack of funding didn't stop the rise of soccer teams such as Orlando Pirates and Kaizer Chiefs.

As a result of its apartheid policies, South African sport was fragmented for decades and the country was isolated from world competition. The year 1991 saw major changes taking place politically and socially in the country and, as a result, the international sporting community once again opened its doors.

In the early days of democracy, one of the most memorable highlights for each and every South African – rugby supporter or not – was South Africa's win in the 1995 Rugby World Cup. It was endorsed by Nelson Mandela himself, wearing a Number 6 jersey, courtesy of then team captain Francois Pienaar.

This momentous occasion had a profound effect on the nation, both emotionally and in terms of its sporting future. However, the extended period of isolation had left many lingering problems in its wake. Because of the lack of international competition, many talents failed to reach their potential and the 'big match temperament' is still lacking in many of the country's major sports. Infighting often blurs the lines between politics and sport and has not been conducive to achieving the best performances on the field.

The question of transformation remains at the heart of sport in South Africa. While integration will take time, financial support and a lot of patience, the major focus is aimed at the country's youth, and programmes have been set up to foster a non-segregated sporting culture among young South Africans. Township training initiatives and facilities are being established, and although progress is slow, South Africa is starting to reap the rewards, with sporting heroes like Mkhaya Ntini (cricket) and Bryan Habana (rugby) having led the way to transformation.

Rugby, cricket and soccer represent the most popular sports in South Africa. Rugby's Springboks showcase their form in stadiums around the world, while the Proteas definitely give international cricketing teams a run for their money.

The beautiful game, however, is arguably the number one spectator sport in South Africa, and its stadiums fill to capacity every Saturday during soccer season. The national team, Bafana Bafana ('The Boys'), united South Africans behind them with their determined performances during the 2010 Fifa World Cup™, which the country hosted.

South Africa is certainly demonstrating its abilities when it comes to swimming and golf. Superstars in the pool, Ryk Neethling and Roland Schoeman, continue to excel at world events – their 2004 Summer Olympics win made every South African proud. On the golfing front, greats such as Retief Goosen and Ernie Els are regular players on international greens. Other exceptional athletes include Natalie du Toit, a one-legged swimmer and role model to the country's youth, and wheelchair-bound Ernst van Dyk, who has won nine Boston Marathons. Both are Laureus award winners who embody the sporting spirit of the new South Africa.

❯ South Africans love their sport and sporting heroes. Soccer, rugby and cricket are the all-time favourites and fans proudly wear their team's colours.

The economy

South Africa has vast natural resources. It has the world's richest repositories of gold, and diamonds are found in huge numbers off the Namaqualand coast, the Northern Cape and at Cullinan near Pretoria. The North West and Limpopo provinces hold the earth's largest deposits of platinum-group metals, as well as massive reserves of high-grade chromium and nickel. Among the 60 or so minerals mined are manganese, asbestos, phosphates, vanadium, fluorspar and andalusite. The oil and natural gas fields are still in the early stages of development, but it is envisaged that their contribution to the country's energy needs will continue to increase.

Telecommunications and broadcasting services are comparable to those of the most advanced industrialised countries. The various regions, cities and suburbs are linked by 754 000 km of roads, more than 100 000 km of which are tarred, and they are used by nearly eight million vehicles. The rail network comprises 36 000 km of track, most of which is electrified. The construction of the Gautrain Rapid Rail Link, completed for the 2010 Soccer World Cup, is the first step towards a new mass-transit system. South African Airways, the national carrier, and close to 50 other airlines connect the country's three international airports with destinations the world over; domestic services and charter companies link the country's major and many of its minor centres. The principal harbours are at Durban (one of the southern hemisphere's largest and busiest), Cape Town, Port Elizabeth, East London (the only river-port), Richards Bay (the leading outlet for bulk commodities), Mossel Bay, and Saldanha Bay.

State-owned Eskom operates 13 coal-fired plants, six hydroelectric, one nuclear, two pumped storage, and two gas-turbine stations, and generates around two-thirds of all power produced in Africa. Coal and petroleum gas are used extensively in the manufacture of synthetic fuels.

South Africa's diverse climatic conditions accommodate a variety of crops, mainly maize, fruit, vegetables, wine and table grapes, sugar cane, and wheat. The national herd comprises 13 million head of cattle and around 25 million sheep, with wool being a valuable export product. The pine plantations of Mpumalanga and the rich trawling grounds of the Cape's west and south coasts sustain thriving forestry and fishing industries. A flourishing informal economy, which includes backyard industries, street vendors and shebeens, generates work opportunities and income, and helps develop much-needed skills and managerial expertise.

Tourism is seen as one of the key growth areas and is, in fact, the fastest-growing industry in the country.

One of the biggest challenges is the HIV/Aids pandemic. While it may be difficult to determine the extent of this impact, it is certain to affect the country both economically and socially.

▶ The heaps of mined-out ore from Johannesburg's gold mines are a reminder of the country's inextricable link to this precious metal.

The land

The combination of South Africa's varied geography and climate has served to create no less than seven vegetation types. The country's desert environment, in the north-western Kalahari region of South Africa, is characterised by minimal and stunted plant cover. Deep-rooted trees, however, are found along dry watercourses and the sandy flats and gravel plains support succulents and lichens. After rain there is often a scattering of ephemeral grasses.

The succulent Karoo is a semi-desert ecosystem that occurs from Lambert's Bay northwards, and inland to Springbok and Calvinia. Rainfall is 50–200 mm per year and the flora is dominated by a rich variety of hardy perennial succulents and small-leaved shrubs.

The Nama-Karoo is the semi-desert of South Africa's central plateau and extends over the greater part of the Western and Northern Cape provinces and north-westwards to Mariental and Rehoboth in Namibia. Rainfall is erratic and averages 125–375 mm a year. The vegetation comprises perennial succulents and low scrub bushes with small drought-resistant leaves and spreading root systems.

Grasslands dominate the interior uplands and rolling plains of Mpumalanga, the Free State, Lesotho, Eastern Cape and inland KwaZulu-Natal. The highveld grasses are short and the terrain supports few indigenous trees, partly due to frost, drought and fire during winter. In lower-lying areas, however, the grasses are taller.

The Mediterranean climate of the south-west and southern Cape, with its predominantly winter rainfall (400–2 000 mm) and hot, dry summers, is ideal for its unique array of plant species known as fynbos. Although indigenous forest remnants survive in the wetter kloofs, fynbos is essentially a fire-adapted heathland consisting of a variety of distinctive plants such as proteas and ericas.

South Africa is not generously endowed with extensive natural forests, although its man-made plantations are among the largest in the world. Small forested areas occur in year-round rainfall areas of the coastal zone and in the wetter parts of Mpumalanga. The largest surviving natural forest is the strip between George and Humansdorp in the southern Cape. This stretch of woodland is strictly protected and is famous for its ironwoods, stinkwoods and yellowwoods. Evergreen subtropical species, such as palms, grow along the hot, humid KwaZulu-Natal coast, where lagoons and estuaries also support mangroves.

South Africa's bushveld vegetation is characteristic of the northern regions of the country. It ranges from the dry, dense bush of the Lowveld to the open parkland of parts of Limpopo Province, where the grassland is studded with umbrella thorn, marula, mopane and baobab trees.

▶ The seemingly barren landscape of the Richtersveld, now a UNESCO World Heritage Site, actually supports an abundance of life and includes two floristic kingdoms, namely the succulent Karoo and Nama-Karoo.

Majestic mountains

Mountain ranges form a fundamental part of the geography of South Africa, stretching in an almost continuous loop from the Soutpansberg in the north-eastern corner, down to the Drakensberg of KwaZulu-Natal, south-west through the folded mountains of the Cape, and up to the Cederberg and Bokkeveldberg of Namaqualand. Much of South Africa's mountain region collectively makes up the Great Escarpment, the rocky divide that separates the high-lying interior plateau from the lower-lying areas that stretch down to the coast in the south and east.

The Drakensberg is an area of high, lonely places where all is silent but for the cries of raptors and noises that betray the presence of antelope, mountain tortoises and tiny ice rats. The lower-lying parts are popular recreational areas, with holiday-makers flocking there to enjoy the region's walks, riding trails and trout fishing.

The folded ranges of the southern Cape are the most geologically interesting of South Africa's mountains. The extraordinary contortions of Meiringspoort, a narrow gorge winding through the Swartberg, is the most dramatic example,

and Spandaukop and Valley Mountain stand sentinel over the bleakly magnificent Valley of Desolation, a panoramic moonscape of semi-arid Karoo plains framed by jagged dolerite crags. The Witteberg, Swartberg, Langeberg and Outeniqua range separate the Little and Great Karoo from the coast.

At the most westerly end of the Cape's folded coastal rampart is the flat-topped massif of Table Mountain, unquestionably South Africa's most famous landmark. Among the most notable upland areas to the north of Cape Town are the Cederberg mountains, which are home to rare endemic varieties of fynbos and provide sanctuary to the mountain leopard.

▶ The Cederberg is popular with hikers and campers as it offers many interesting trails to explore. ▶ The Swartberg Mountains (overleaf) between the Little Karoo towns of Calitzdorp and Oudtshoorn are often dusted with snow during the winter months.

Flowers in the dust

Although South Africa is predominantly dry, vegetation is able to thrive in some of the unlikeliest places. This is especially true in Namaqualand and the north-western Cape where the indigenous plants have evolved fascinating strategies to survive. For some plants the only source of water comes from the dense fog that moves in off the sea, while others have adapted to the extreme heat and drought by means of moisture-retentive stems and leaves, or by means of bulbs, corms and tubers that lie buried beneath the soil.

The region is also home to swiftly flowering ephemerals, which avoid drought by remaining dormant in seed form until the rains come. They then germinate rapidly, grow, flower, and again survive the dry summer in the form of seed. In their short life they produce brilliant flower shows for hundreds of kilometres from just north of Cape Town up through to Namaqualand. From mid-August to late September and October the region is transformed into a sea of flowers and visitors arrive in busloads to witness this multi-coloured spectacle. For the remainder of the year, the landscape reverts to its cover of dwarf shrubs and sturdy succulents, including the cleverly disguised stone flowers, or Lithops.

The Richtersveld hosts an exceptional variety of succulents and where the succulent Karoo vegetation gives way to that of the Nama-Karoo, a variety of euphorbias punctuate the landscape, including the *halfmens* tree, which faces forever into the blazing sun. Aloes are also found here, as is the *kokerboom* or quiver tree, which dominates from vantage points on stony hillcrests.

The red dunes of the Kalahari in the extreme north-west of the country are home to sweet grasses and acacias, including the camel thorn, which provides valuable shade and fodder from its leaves, seed pods and gum. The nara melon, which lies partly concealed in the sand, is a vital source of water in this arid landscape.

▶ Namaqualand's springtime floral displays draw thousands of visitors each year from all around the world.

Coast of contrasts

South Africa's coastline stretches for more than 3 000 km and is washed by two of the world's great oceans – the Atlantic along the west coast and south-western tip, and the Indian along the south and east coasts. It is a shoreline of dramatic contrasts, ranging from long white beaches to sheer rocky cliffs. Formidable winds and currents often cause tempestuous seas that have resulted in no less than 3 000 shipwrecks along and off the country's shores.

The coastal margin is well defined and consists of three distinctive coastal zones: the arid west coast, the temperate south-east coast and the warm subtropical east coast. The whole of South Africa's west coast abuts the Atlantic Ocean and the cold Benguela Current gives this stretch a combination of oceanographic and weather phenomena that make it the country's most important commercial fishing region. Remote harbours, protected lagoons, and seal and seabird colonies punctuate the West Coast and, despite its harsh environment and starkly sculpted landscapes, it is a region much loved by the people who live there.

Although it is the view of oceanographers that the Atlantic and Indian oceans meet at Cape Agulhas, there is no immediate change here from cold to warm water. Instead, the change occurs gradually over the 1 000-km stretch from Hermanus eastwards to Port St Johns. The warm, subtropical conditions of the Indian Ocean from Port St Johns to Maputaland and beyond, and the warm Mozambique and Agulhas currents, provide an aquatic world of crystal waters and coral reefs. It is along this stretch of coastline that South Africa's abundant bathing, water sports and sailing activities are concentrated.

Conservation is a priority along South Africa's coastline and, in order to safeguard and preserve the marine environment for future generations, 19 marine and adjacent onshore conservation areas are protected. iSimangaliso Wetland Park, formerly known as the Greater St Lucia Wetland Park, was declared a UNESCO World Heritage Site in 1999 and consists of eight interlinked ecosystems, making this one of the world's most biologically rich reserves. Other important marine reserves include the Tsitsikamma section of the Garden Route National Park, De Hoop Marine Protected Area and the Aliwal Shoal.

Migrating southern right and humpback whales, which come into local waters to mate and calve each year, are also protected and whale-watching is very popular along the western and southern seaboards, particularly from June to November.

▶ South Africa has more than 3 000 km of coastline, ranging from the subtropical regions of the east coast to the stark beauty of the west coast.

The wild kingdom

There's little to equal the adrenalin charge of seeing wild animals in their natural habitat, and Africa is undisputably the best place to do it. South Africa, which occupies a mere one per cent of the earth's land surface, is home to no less than six per cent – 227 species – of the world's mammals, not to mention a huge diversity of birds, fish, reptiles, amphibians, insects, plants and flowers.

Most of the country's national parks and well-appointed private reserves boast one or more of the Big Five – buffalo, lion, leopard, rhino and elephant – but it is within the sanctuary of the 20 000-km² world-renowned Kruger National Park that visitors can be certain of seeing the greatest number of big game animals.

▶ The Big Five – rhino, buffalo (also overleaf), lion, elephant and leopard – are what visitors hope to see on a visit to South Africa's game parks and reserves.

It is also one of only three reserves in South Africa where the endangered wild dog can be found. Besides the Kruger, other major wildlife sanctuaries include the Kgalagadi Transfrontier Park in the far Northern Cape and south-western corner of Botswana, the Addo National Park in the Eastern Cape, the Hluhluwe-Imfolozi Park in KwaZulu-Natal, which is home to the world's largest concentration of white rhino, Maputaland's Ndumu reserve, and the vast iSimangaliso complex of forest, lake, estuarine, marine and terrestrial reserves.

Game-viewing in South Africa is generally best during the cooler winter months (June to August) when grass is short and lack of water lures game to the waterholes, but some visitors prefer early summer (November and December) when wildebeest, impala and other species give birth and great numbers of migrant birds are present.

Birdlife

South Africa has a rich and varied avifauna with close to 900 species, but for the visitor who wants to achieve a good list of birds, it is essential to set aside enough time to sample as many habitats as possible.

The coastline and nutrient-rich offshore waters of South Africa attract species ranging from albatrosses and petrels that breed on subantarctic islands, or even Antarctica itself, to the African penguin, the only penguin that breeds on the African continent. To tick off some of the deep-sea species, enthusiasts would have to charter a boat and travel out to sea.

An endemic species is one confined to a particular region or habitat, and there are close to 100 endemic birds in South Africa. Most of the central and western regions are arid and it is here that many endemics occur, particularly among groups such as korhaans and larks. The Cape Floral Kingdom of the Western Cape is also home to several endemics, including the Cape sugarbird, orange-breasted sunbird, Cape siskin and protea canary. There are almost 70 species of diurnal birds of prey, ranging from the crowned eagle to the pygmy falcon, as well as 12 species of owl. For raptor enthusiasts, South Africa is a treasure-trove in which endemics such as the Cape vulture and black harrier are a particular attraction.

It is impossible in a brief account to highlight the many birds, but wherever visitors find themselves in South Africa, they will have a good birdwatching day.

▶ Pied kingfisher (above), southern carmine bee-eater and gannet (opposite top and bottom) are but three of 900 species of birds found in South Africa.

Johannesburg skyline at night.

From Africa's powerhouse to the cradle of humankind

Gauteng, entirely rural until just over a century ago, was impelled into the modern era with the discovery of gold on the Witwatersrand in 1886, an event which gave birth to the city of Johannesburg. Since then many other minerals have been discovered in the area and are being profitably exploited, making Gauteng the wealthiest province in South Africa and the second most populated.

Johannesburg, also known as Egoli or 'place of gold', is Gauteng's capital. It is a densely packed, sophisticated, high-rise metropolis and the powerhouse of Africa. Soweto, developed as a township during the apartheid years but now a city within a city, is home to around two million people and is a popular tourist destination. Pretoria, 50 km to the north of Johannesburg, is the capital of South Africa where the Union Buildings and other historic buildings are a key attraction.

Although much of Gauteng is highly urbanised, it also includes the Cradle of Humankind World Heritage Site, the Sterkfontein caves, Maropeng and wetlands of international significance. It is also an area with a rich cultural heritage, and the setting for much of the struggle against apartheid.

Most of the Witwatersrand's early mines have long since been worked out, leaving only their rusting headgear and dumps as a reminder of those rugged pioneering days. Mining operations have moved to the East and West Rand areas to either side of the city and the mines tunnel an immense distance beneath the surface of the Highveld. South Africa, which is believed to have around 40% of the world's gold reserves, produces about 14% of the world's gold each year.

The Johannesburg Securities Exchange, a gleaming modern building of glass and steel in Sandton, is but one example of contemporary architecture that reflects the city's thriving financial, commercial and industrial centre. But there is also a wealth of culture to be enjoyed and visitors can experience the many theatres, art galleries and museums found throughout this dynamic city.

Contrasts! Johannesburg is full of them. It is this eclectic mix that contributes to today's exciting, multi-cultural city. Modern skyscrapers in downtown Johannesburg stand alongside pavement stalls, *muti* shops and the few authentic relics of Victoriana left untouched by modern developers. The old Indian fruit and vegetable market has happily been preserved: it escaped destruction by being converted into the Market Theatre. Situated in the Newtown Cultural Precinct, the Market Theatre plays a major cultural role in South Africa's performing arts. Renowned worldwide for staging anti-apartheid plays – including *Sophiatown* and *Bopha* – the theatre continues to play a role in developing the best of South African theatre, music, dance and other related arts.

Not too far from Johannesburg's city centre is the Apartheid Museum. Built close to one of the city's big tourist attractions – Gold Reef City – this museum is the opposite of the glitz and glamour of the nearby theme park and casino. The world-class Apartheid Museum offers a melancholy journey into South Africa's turbulent apartheid history. Dedicated to the country's struggle heroes and the triumph of the human spirit over adversity, the exhibits take a long and sobering look at the apartheid policies entrenched by the National Party after it came to power in 1948. More than 20 exhibition areas take the visitor on a journey from the early days of segregation to the formalising of apartheid, the rise of Black Consciousness, and then they deliver the observer to the final phases of long-awaited freedom for all South Africans.

Zoo Lake is a man-made body of water bordered by weeping willows and set in rolling lawns. It is a tranquil weekend picnic spot where you can hire a rowing boat or where children can feed the ducks. The nearby Johannesburg Zoo is also a popular attraction. Night tours, which enable visitors to witness the lively nocturnal activities of owls, bushbabies and hyaenas, are available.

Johannesburg has extensive, world-class sports complexes. The Wanderers Cricket Stadium hosts regular international cricketing events, while Coca-Cola Park Stadium (formerly known as Ellis Park) is one of the country's premier rugby, soccer and concert venues. South Africa hosted the 2010 Soccer World Cup and new stadiums were built and existing ones upgraded to accommodate the world's greatest soccer-playing nations and the influx of soccer fans. The FNB Stadium (also known as Soccer City) was used as the main venue and hosted the opening and final matches of this international competition.

▶ The city of Johannesburg, also known as Egoli, or the City of Gold, has been indelibly linked with this precious metal since the discovery of the main reef in 1886.

▶ The Montecasino development is one of Gauteng's premier gaming, retail and leisure complexes.

▶ Melrose Arch, a multi-use precinct that combines office, commercial and residential developments in one area, reflects Gauteng's urban lifestyle.

Soweto, once at the forefront of the liberation struggle in South Africa, is now a popular tourist destination. A tourism and information centre has been built to assist the thousands of visitors who come here every month, and numerous bed-and-breakfast enterprises and guest houses have sprung up to accommodate the tourists who come from across the world to see this vibrant city and meet its people. Sightseeing tours usually include visits to the house where Nelson Mandela lived before he was jailed, Walter Sisulu Square, where the Freedom Charter was signed and adopted in 1955, the Regina Mundi Catholic Church, and the Hector Pieterson Museum. This museum, and the Hector Pieterson Memorial, commemorate the uprising that took place in Soweto on 16 June 1976 when close to 20 000 students protested against the apartheid education system. Hector Pieterson was the first of many students shot dead by the police on that fateful day.

Pretoria, the nation's capital, is well known for its jacarandas, which are best admired from the elevated gardens of the Union Buildings during their short springtime flowering season. The buildings, designed by Sir Herbert Baker, serve as offices for the departments of the State President and Foreign Affairs.

The National Zoological Gardens of South Africa in Pretoria are the largest in the country and cover about 80 ha. Visitors can experience the zoo by joining one of the tour options – on foot, boarding the cableway, or chugging slowly past the camps on a tractor-train. The zoo combines its entertainment function with considerable emphasis on conservation, education and research.

Freedom Park, situated on Salvokop south of Pretoria's CBD, lies within view of the Union Buildings and the Voortrekker Monument, and has been established as a symbol of the struggle for freedom and humanity in South Africa, as well as a symbol of reconciliation and a link between past and present. A Wall of Names and eternal flame commemorate those who died in the struggle against apartheid.

Forty kilometres north-west of Pretoria is the 1.4-km-diameter, 200-m-deep Tswaing Meteorite Crater, the result of a meteorite impact 220 000 years ago. An extensive wetland system and about 240 bird species can also be seen at the site.

Maropeng and the Sterkfontein Caves, situated in an area known as the Cradle of Humankind, are a must-see. Significant discoveries of animal and hominid fossils at the caves are a link to the earliest origins of humankind and our evolution. The Hartbeespoort Dam, with its extensive fishing and boating facilities, and the De Wildt Cheetah Research Centre are other popular destinations for day excursions from Pretoria and Johannesburg. Other ways to see the area are to travel on an authentic steam train (affectionately known as the Magaliesberg Express), or for those who really want to get the area into perspective, to take a ride in a hot-air balloon.

Sheltered in a long-extinct volcano, one of only two alkali craters in the world, lies Sun City, an oasis of pleasure unequalled anywhere in Africa. The resort has an amazing range of attractions, from gaming at the casinos and spectacular live shows to the annual golf championship that attracts the world's top golfers. The most fascinating aspect of Sun City is The Lost City and its remarkable Palace Hotel, surrounded by 25 ha of rare and beautiful gardens. It overlooks the Valley of Waves and dominates the skyline with its majestic towers of imitation elephant tusks.

The Pilanesberg National Park, which borders Sun City, covers 55 000 ha of natural bush that serves as home to the Big Five. It lies in a bowl encircled by concentric rings of volcanic hills 1 200 million years old, and its natural amphi-theatres provide excellent game-viewing opportunities. The park is a meeting point of the High- and Lowveld, so it is one of the few reserves where springbok and impala naturally cohabit. The mixed sourveld vegetation and variety of trees, interspersed with numerous waterholes, support a large variety of game and birds, and the Mankwe Dam is home to hippo, crocodile and many waterbirds.

▶ Johannesburg is a modern city that has earned its reputation as Africa's powerhouse. Contemporary engineering and architecture, such as that of the Nelson Mandela Bridge (above) and Diagonal Street's skyscrapers (right), keep pace with the city's vibrant CBD.

▶ The Apartheid Museum is one of Johannesburg's top tourist destinations, but it also serves as a monument to the men and women who struggled against the injustices of apartheid. It is a poignant reminder of the triumph of the human spirit over adversity.

▶ Pretoria is the capital of South Africa and home to the Union Buildings and many other architectural gems. But the city is equally renowned for its jacaranda trees (left), which put on a beautiful display each spring. ▶ The Sterkfontein Caves (above) are found in an area known as the Cradle of Humankind, where the discovery of thousands of hominid and animal fossils is helping scientists piece together the story of human evolution. The area has been proclaimed a World Heritage Site.

◗ The Hartbeespoort Dam, set against the backdrop of the Magaliesberg, is a popular weekend and day trip destination for Gauteng families. Activities include a variety of water sports, as well as hang-gliding and paragliding. You can even take a trip in a hot-air balloon (overleaf).

▶ The Valley of the Waves at the Lost City, Sun City (left). This entertainment and leisure complex, known as Africa's kingdom of pleasure, offers visitors gaming, live entertainment, water sports, world-renowned golf courses and many other family-orientated activities. ▶ The Lesedi Cultural Village (above) not far from Sun City gives visitors insight into the cultural wealth of the Zulu, Xhosa, Pedi, Sotho and Ndebele people of South Africa.

▶ Buffalo, often called the most dangerous of the Big Five, come down to drink at a water hole in the Kruger National Park.

Kruger National Park and the Great Escarpment

Roughly 400 km long by 150 km wide, the Lowveld sprawls across the north-eastern corner of South Africa between Zimbabwe, Swaziland, Mozambique and the Great Escarpment.

When the eastern Lowveld was still wild and undeveloped, the discovery of gold around Pilgrim's Rest lured tens of thousands of fortune-seekers to the region. As there were no towns or shops, the speculators hunted for their food, and animals in the area were decimated. After the eastern gold rush fizzled out, President Paul Kruger urged his parliament to create a sanctuary to protect the remaining wildlife of the Lowveld. In 1898, some 4 600 km² between the Sabie and Umgwenya (Crocodile) rivers were proclaimed the Sabie Game Reserve. That was the birth of the Kruger National Park. In 1903 a second reserve was proclaimed, the Shingwedzi, which encompassed the land further north between the Letaba and the Limpopo rivers. In 1926 both reserves, and the farmland between them, were consolidated into the Kruger National Park. Later still, more land was added and the reserve reached its present size of about 20 000 km².

While the park is not the largest of its kind, it is recognised as the world's leader in African fauna and flora research and in environmental management. It also offers the average person the chance of observing an unequalled variety of wildlife at close proximity. Its facilities include a range of accommodation from lodges and bungalows to huts and camping, restaurants, shops, an education centre, a library, and an expansive network of good roads.

Future developments for Kruger include its incorporation into the Great Limpopo Transfrontier Park. This initiative will link Kruger with the Limpopo National Park in Mozambique, and Gonarezhou National Park, Manjinji Pan Sanctuary and Malipati Safari Area in Zimbabwe. Large sections of fencing must be dismantled between the three countries, and only once there is free movement of people and animals within the park can it be officially opened. While steps have been taken in this direction, it will still take a number of years before the park comes into existence.

The southern half of the Kruger National Park is the oldest and most accessible part and has more accommodation, roads, picnic places and viewpoints than the northern half. The park is crisscrossed by rivers and streams fringed with trees, but away from the rivers the land changes from acacia woodland to scrub and grassy plains, home to sable, rhino, waterbuck, duiker, buffalo, impala, wildebeest and zebra. Here too are predators such as lion, cheetah, wild dog, hyaena and jackal.

Skukuza, the oldest camp, is on the Sabie River. It is the focal point of the southern region and a veritable town. Pretoriuskop, the fourth largest camp, is where transport wagons paused on their way to and from Delagoa Bay in the past. The old route, plied by Sir Percy Fitzpatrick and other intrepid men, is clearly signposted and nearby Jock Safari Lodge is named after Fitzpatrick's famed dog, Jock of the Bushveld. The Lower Sabie and Crocodile Bridge camps have large shade trees and are known for their birdlife. Berg-en-Dal camp blends in with its bushveld surroundings and wilderness trails lead walkers to a profusion of San rock paintings.

Satara, well north of Skukuza, is a large circular camp in extensive bushy plains that teem with game, often seen in huge herds. Farther north still, Olifants camp, perched high on a ridge, has superb views across the Lepelle (Olifants) River.

In hunter tradition, the Big Five are elephant, rhino, lion, leopard and buffalo; they are the most sought-after and are all found in the Lowveld. But why only these five? The reason is that the Big Five are the most dangerous; other mammals are seldom as dangerous unless they are cornered. The elephant, for instance, is immensely powerful and makes a terrifying opponent when challenged or wounded. The rhino, especially the black variety, is notoriously bad-tempered when aroused and unstoppable when it charges. Demand for its horn in the Middle and Far East has led to its virtual extermination in much of Africa, but the Kruger's population is well protected and has shown steady growth since its reintroduction. Lion are extremely strong and fast, and so are leopard, which are also stealthy. Finally, the Cape buffalo, when wounded, cunningly ambushes its pursuer and wields its huge curved horns with awesome, single-minded power.

For the purists there is little to match the natural treasures of the Kruger Park's northern half. From the Lepelle River to the vicinity of the Zimbabwe border, mixed mopane scrub and forest stretch as far as the eye can see, an ocean of pale green in summer, a rich glowing red in winter, and grey in times of drought. Around the jungle-like reaches of the Luvuvhu River, flowers and creepers form spectacular displays along riverbanks teeming with birds, and rare roan antelope, nyala and shy bushbuck can be seen.

Letaba restcamp is a cool oasis graced by bird-rich subtropical growth which overlooks a wide bend in the Letaba River. Animals go there to drink, and two nearby dams also provide game and waterbird viewing sites.

Shingwedzi camp lies beside a river of the same name and is popular because many kinds of animals tend to stroll by casually. Downstream from the camp is the Kanniedood Dam, where you can watch hippos and waterbirds from log hides.

Punda Maria camp, spread across the flank of a bushy hill, derives half its name from the Swahili word for zebra – *punda milia* – and the other half from the wife

▶ The historic village of Pilgrim's Rest, a remnant of the area's gold rush.

of the ranger who established the camp. Sable favour this area and can often be admired from a distance. Near the camp the view sweeps over hills and valleys blanketed by a dense growth of trees, shrubs, creepers and grasses.

Punda Maria is the nearest camp to what many visitors believe to be the most entrancing part of the park – Pafuri. The road leading to it descends through mopane and baobab trees into the shallow valley of the Luvuvhu River. Side roads lead you into riverine forest, a mix of jackalberry, nyala, leadwood, sausage, ana, fever and many other trees that spread a canopy of dappled green high over the still surface of the river. Hundreds of different kinds of birds dwell in the green reaches, among them Cape parrot, Narina trogon, hornbill, crested guineafowl, barbet, gorgeous bush shrike, boubou and Pel's fishing owl.

Apart from the Kruger National Park, there are scores of smaller reserves in the Lowveld. The biggest and best are located along Kruger's western boundary, and are so well run that the park has dismantled its fences to allow its animals to move freely around the wider area.

The Great Escarpment, the northern segment of South Africa's Drakensberg, is a wall of mountain towering up to 1 200 m above the Lowveld bush from Zimbabwe to Swaziland and, for sheer scenic beauty, few parts of Africa can compare with this region. In Limpopo Province near the border with Zimbabwe live the VhaVenda. Theirs is a land of tribal legend, remote reserves and wonders hidden in secret valleys. The fresh waters of the sacred Lake Fundudzi are believed to reject impurities, and the forests of giant hardwoods, a burial ground of tribal chiefs, have ancient ruins scattered here and there.

As the Escarpment approaches Tzaneen, the roads twist down through Magoebaskloof, which boasts the Escarpment's largest patch of indigenous forest, and Duiwelskloof, past fruit orchards, chilly trout streams and natural woodland. In the Modjadji Nature Reserve, successive generations of rain queens protect the forest of giant cycads. The 16-km-long and 600-m-deep Blyde River Canyon is also in the area. Upstream on the Motlatse (Blyde) River are the Bourke's Luck Potholes, where stones churned by water have carved a filigree of weirdly eroded rock.

Above the Escarpment rim you find Pilgrim's Rest, a fascinating village of corrugated-iron shops and houses, looking still much as it did during the gold rush over a century ago. Near Pilgrim's Rest is God's Window, where the 1 500-m-high Escarpment plunges in an almost sheer drop to the Lowveld below.

The Lowveld Escarpment is laced with waterfalls. One spectacular and easily reached cataract is at the point where the Elands River plunges from Emgwenya (Waterval Boven) into a gorge beside the main road, down to Waterval Onder. Other falls worth a visit are Sabie Falls, and the Lone Creek, Horseshoe and Bridal Veil cascades. In the Pilgrim's Rest area are the twin columns of the famed Mac-Mac Falls, which drop straight down into the pool far below.

▶ The Magoebaskloof region in Limpopo is a green haven of farmlands, indigenous forests and cultivated tree plantations. The area is also renowned for the variety of outdoor activities it offers visitors.

Gold has been part of the story of southern Africa for at least 2 000 years. The precious metal was in common use many centuries ago and the treasures of a vanished people – beads, bracelets and other ornaments – were discovered on a low flat hill named Mapungubwe in the Limpopo Province. The Mapungubwe Cultural Landscape, the remains of what was once the largest kingdom on the subcontinent until it was abandoned in the fourteenth century, is a UNESCO World Heritage Site. The modern quest for gold began in earnest around the middle of the nineteenth century. When it was discovered near Mashishing (formerly Lydenburg) and near the Letaba River, it triggered a frantic rush, and tent and shack settlements mushroomed around Spitskop, Mac-Mac and Pilgrim's Rest. But the alluvial gold ran out and the populations of these 'instant' towns dwindled. The biggest strikes were around present-day Barberton. The Sheba reef, at the time ranked as the world's richest mine, was discovered in the nearby mountains. While the glory days of the town have passed, the mine is still going strong today.

The walks and hiking trails of the Escarpment cover hundreds of kilometres and are remarkably varied. The Thate Vondo Hiking Trail takes you through commercial plantations, indigenous forest and to the sacred locations of the Fundudzi lake and the Thate Vondo Forest. The Jock of the Bushveld Trail runs close to the edge of the Kruger Park and is a five-day route on which hikers are able to see plenty of big game. The Fanie Botha Hiking Trail runs between the Ceylon State Forest and God's Window and can be completed in one five-day or two- or three-day hikes.

Mpumalanga is known across the world for its superb game parks and reserves, most notably the Kruger National Park. Many of the area's private reserves, such as Mala Mala (above) and Sabi Sabi (right), offer visitors the ultimate in luxury accommodation and outstanding game-viewing with highly trained and knowledgeable guides. The Kruger National Park is one of South Africa's main tourist destinations and is well geared to cater for the constant flow of visitors. Accommodation options range from camping and bungalows to exclusive camps, such as Bateleur bushveld camp near the Rooibosrand Dam (overleaf).

▶ A lioness stalks her prey in the Kruger National Park (left). The park has a large predator population, with lions numbering around 1 500. Kruger is home to nearly 145 mammal species, including baboons (above), and more than 500 species of birds. ▶ A golden sunrise near Pretoriuskop camp in the Kruger National Park (overleaf).

Waterfalls are scattered across the Lowveld Escarpment and while some are only accessible on hiking trails, others – such as the Horseshoe Falls (above) near Sabie and the Lisbon Falls (right) near Graskop – are easily reached after a short walk.

▶ The view over Blydepoort Dam in the Blyde River Canyon.

The Drakensberg

▶ The Amphitheatre, the most recognisable section of the Drakensberg, dominates the Royal Natal Park.

Scenic highlands and mountain retreats

The gigantic rampart of mountains known as the Drakensberg is the highest and scenically most spectacular part of the Great Escarpment that fringes South Africa's 3 000-km coastal belt. It also forms a natural divide between KwaZulu-Natal in the east and Lesotho and the Free State in the west.

The range is at its loftiest in the kingdom of Lesotho, where it is known as the Maluti mountains. To the west and north of the Malutis is the great plateau of the Free State, a fertile countryside that rises to picturesquely weathered hills, of which those in the Golden Gate Highlands National Park are strikingly colourful.

The strange configurations of the hills of the eastern Free State are as varied as the shades of their sediment layers. Among the largest of the flat-topped bastions is Thaba Nchu (black mountain), which lies between Bloemfontein and Lesotho. Closer to the KwaZulu-Natal border is the Kerkenberg (church mountain), named by the Voortrekkers who camped in its shadow before venturing into the Drakensberg, while the oddest of the configurations is the Tandjiesberg, whose contours are reminiscent of a set of giant teeth.

The ancient plains of the Free State contain numerous sedimentary layers and extensive fossil beds have been uncovered. Fossilised dinosaur footprints can be found near Ladybrand, and a number of dinosaur egg nests containing fossil embryos have also been uncovered in the Golden Gate Highlands National Park. The park can lay just claim to its name when the layered orange and yellow sandstone comes to life in the setting sun. The mountainous landscape of the 11 600-ha park rises from 1 892 m at its lowest point to 2 770 m at its highest. In the natural highland vegetation of sour grasses, herbs and shrubs, there is an abundance of indigenous wildlife, including black wildebeest, eland, grey rhebok, oribi, red hartebeest, blesbok, mountain reedbuck and zebra. There is also plenty for birdwatchers to study, from large raptors and blue cranes to the rare bearded vulture and bald ibis.

The Drakensberg mountain range stretches from Stormberg in the Eastern Cape, right up to the border between northern KwaZulu-Natal and Mpumalanga. The Voortrekkers who first saw the mountains named them the Drache Berg because their jagged edges and isolated pinnacles gave the impression of the ridged back of a dragon. The Zulu, on the other hand, call them *uKhahlamba*, or 'the barrier of spears'. Both names convey the impression of an impenetrable rampart. In the haze of a hot summer's day the Drakensberg appears blue and distant. As winter approaches and the air clears, the snow-capped mountains stand out, sharply silhouetted against the bright sky.

The uKhahlamba-Drakensberg Park, a World Heritage Site encompassing 243 000 ha, stretches from Bushman's Neck in the south to the Royal Natal Park in the north. The park has a rich natural and cultural heritage, being home to a number of rare and endangered species of birds as well as protecting the richest concentration of San rock paintings in South Africa.

The Drakensberg has many features. Mont-aux-Sources in the Royal Natal Park, on the northern boundary of the mountain wall, marks the fifth highest point in the range, standing at 3 282 m. Four rivers rise on this 'mountain of springs', including two of South Africa's largest – the Orange, which runs west, and the eastward-flowing Tugela. The Injisuthi Dome on the northern border of Giant's Castle Nature Reserve stands at 3 410 m and marks the highest point in the South African Drakensberg. (Thabana Ntlenyana is the highest point in Africa south of Kilimanjaro and lies inside the Lesotho border.) Giant's Castle itself, at 3 314 m, is the fourth highest peak. About midway along the wall the massive 3 004-m Cathedral Peak dominates the landscape.

The uKhahlamba-Drakensberg Park is a popular year-round destination with local and foreign tourists. It has a range of accommodation options and facilities and its rock art, walks, hiking trails and fly-fishing for trout are the main drawcards.

The Drakensberg is home to around 300 species of birds, including the rare bearded vulture. In order to encourage public interest in the species and its habits, an observation hide has been built in the Giant's Castle Reserve. It is open only

▶ Brandwag rock in the Golden Gate Highlands National Park in the Free State.

during winter, the birds' non-breeding season, but allows visitors superb views of this species, and of other vultures and birds of prey that live in the area.

The Drakensberg's passes are as spectacular as its peaks and parks. Some, like the Organ Pipes Pass, are mere tracks; others are faint, perilously steep paths used only by intrepid hikers. There are four national road passes that cut through the Escarpment on the northern borders of KwaZulu-Natal to reach Mpumalanga and the Free State. It is the route that leads up to the mountain kingdom of Lesotho, however, that provides the visitor with the most memorable experience. The switchback corners of the Sani Pass take you 2 865 m up to the highest pub in South Africa.

To the east, the Drakensberg's craggy slopes give way to the rolling hills and misty valleys of the KwaZulu-Natal Midlands, a beautiful and peaceful-looking land whose grasses once sustained huge herds of plains game. The beauty and tranquillity, however, are deceptive, as the region served as a battleground for much of the nineteenth century.

First there was Shaka who, in forging his Zulu empire, caused the blood of unknown thousands to be shed, and the inter-tribal wars, known as the *mfecane* (the crushing), raged across the eastern and northern part of southern Africa for over a decade.

▶ Banks of cosmos flower in late summer and autumn to brighten up the landscape of the Golden Gate Highlands National Park and the north-eastern Free State.

Thereafter followed many clashes between Voortrekker and Zulu, the British and Zulu, and the Voortrekker and British. The various battlefields – most notably Isandlwana, Rorke's Drift, Ulundi, Blood River (now the Mulaudzi River), Talana Hill, Colenso, and Spioenkop – are scattered all over the landscape of rural KwaZulu-Natal and the Battlefield Routes are visited by thousands every year. Stone forts are dotted about the countryside and there are several museums telling the stories of the battles and containing many of the relics of these historic events.

Wrapped in the folds of the hills of the Midlands are numerous villages and towns with names that reflect the origins of their various inhabitants. There are places named after the English aristocracy and countryside, recalling the area's colonial history, while others point to the Zulu presence; Ixopo, for example, is a name derived from the squelching sound made by cattle plodding through mud.

Once it has been seen, the Valley of a Thousand Hills will never be forgotten. The huge valley, carved by the Mgeni River, runs down from a point near Pietermaritzburg to the coast close to the city of Durban. The Midlands Meander, an arts and crafts route just north of Pietermaritzburg, is a key attraction in this region. A diverse mix of crafts are on offer, including weaving, pottery, woodcrafts, cheese-making and beer-brewing.

KwaZulu-Natal is blessed with at least 20 major watercourses and innumerable streams, which have carved the underlying sandstone into sheer-sided valleys and magnificent gorges. One such cleft is the Oribi Gorge on the Mzimkulwana River. It is 24 km long, 5 km wide and 400 m deep and is situated in the Oribi Gorge Nature Reserve, which provides sanctuary to many mammals and birds. The Mgeni River and its tributaries are the main source of water for the two major urban areas of the province. The river reaches the Indian Ocean at Blue Lagoon in Durban, and its course is blocked by four major dams in the hills overlooking Pietermaritzburg. One of these, the Midmar, has been turned into a popular holiday resort by the provincial conservation agency Ezemvelo KwaZulu-Natal Wildlife. The resort offers a variety of recreational attractions, as well as accommodation in chalets and at a caravan park. Bathing can be enjoyed in a large swimming pool, or in the dam, the venue for the annual Midmar Mile, a swimming race that attracts hundreds of entrants. In the adjacent nature reserve visitors can view varied and abundant wildlife, including zebra and white rhino.

The Tugela River is KwaZulu-Natal's mightiest river and one of the largest in South Africa. It originates high up the Drakensberg at Mont-aux-Sources and, within the first few kilometres of its source, it drops in a series of spectacular, ribbon-like cascades, known as the Tugela Falls. The rapids in the gorge below the falls offer superior whitewater rafting.

KwaZulu-Natal's rivers are the venues for two important canoe races – the Duzi, which attracts around 2 000 participants, and the Umkomaas, the country's longest distance race over two days.

Another great sporting event is the Comrades Marathon, which every year attracts thousands of runners and joggers from around the world to test themselves against the 90 km of hills and valleys that divide Pietermaritzburg and Durban.

▶ The many peaks of the Drakensberg, including the Sentinel (above), Monk's Cowl, Injisuthi and the seemingly unclimbable Devil's Tooth, lure mountain and rock climbers from around the world to test their skills.

▶ The snow-covered peaks of the Drakensberg during winter (right).

▶ Scenic Giant's Castle in the uKhahlamba-Drakensberg Park is very popular with hikers. There is also a good chance of seeing the rare bearded vulture here.

▶ The Drakensberg is also the playground of adventure sports enthusiasts, who can enjoy river kayaking during the summer months and ice climbing in winter.

The scenic beauty and tranquillity of the Royal Natal Park (above) makes it a popular holiday destination with both local and overseas visitors. For those with an interest in history, there are many battlefields to explore, and a visit to the Blood River Monument (opposite top left) is a must. Birders will also find much to do here, and a chance to tick off the rare bearded vulture (opposite top right) or Cape rock-thrush (opposite centre) is not to be missed. The Sani Valley (opposite) is a good destination for fly-fishing enthusiasts. ▶ The peaks of the majestic Drakensberg, or 'mountains of the dragon', rise up above the clouds (overleaf).

▶ Giant's Castle forms the backdrop to this typical KwaZulu-Natal rural scene.

Golden sands, battlefields and game parks

From Durban, the largest and busiest port in Africa, KwaZulu-Natal's Indian Ocean shoreline stretches north to the remoteness of the Mozambique border and south to the land of the Xhosa. It is a coast stunning in its beauty and diversity, a 550-km compound of blue sea, exquisite little coves, lagoons and estuaries, golden beaches, lushly evergreen hinterland, wetlands, forest, and superb game reserves that, together, make the region one of the southern hemisphere's most entrancing tourist destinations. This is also the country of the Zulu, harsh in its history, but always vibrant and colourful.

Durban, often referred to as the playground of the Zulu kingdom, is a vibrant city made up of different peoples and cultures, a mix of South Africans of mainly Zulu, British and Indian descent. The city's colonial heritage is reflected in a number of elegant buildings from that era, and stores, heady with the aromas of curry spices and powders, are indicative of the Indian influence and descendants of the indentured labourers who came to these shores in 1860 to work the sugar plantations. Durban is a modern city and thriving commercial centre, but it is also the holiday destination of choice for thousands of local and foreign visitors. Sun-drenched beaches, top-class accommodation, restaurants, and a diverse range of land- and water-based activities mean tourists are spoilt for choice.

For those wanting to explore the cultural aspects of the city, there are annual dance, film and poetry festivals on offer. Museums worth a visit include the Kwa-Muhle Museum, which once housed the Department of Native Affairs but now documents Durban's history, the Durban Cultural and Documentation Centre, which shows the historical and cultural development of the Indian community, and the offbeat Time Warp Museum, which is dedicated to the history of surfing.

Mahatma Ghandi has firm roots in South Africa, and particularly Durban, because it was here that he began his political career and philosophy of non-violence. His continued fight against injustice ultimately led to the liberation of India from British occupation. Sarvodaya, the home where Ghandi lived in Phoenix, a settlement he established, is situated 15 km from central Durban and is visited daily by tourists and locals.

In Durban the seasons make little difference. The shores of the Golden Mile lie in the subtropics and are washed by the warm Mozambique Current. This means that even in winter temperatures seldom fall below 15 °C, while in the summer months they reach well into the thirties. The Golden Mile begins on the seaward side of a spit of land known as the Point, which separates Durban harbour from the Indian Ocean. Addington Beach is the first of the Golden Mile's sandy stretches and is followed by Pumphouse Beach, where tourists leave the waves to surfers and skiers, and are treated, in return, to a daily display of impressive skill and daring. South Beach is extremely popular because of its spaciousness. African arts and crafts can be purchased along the beachfront and, at North Beach, wildlife enthusiasts can enjoy a visit to Fitzsimmons Snake Park.

At the end of the Golden Mile is uShaka Marine World which, at 15 ha, is the largest marine theme park in Africa. This is an ideal destination for a family outing, and facilities include restaurants, a shopping complex, and a variety of water slides in the Wet 'n Wild zone. The key attractions are the dolphinarium and aquarium (one of the five largest in the world), and special viewing windows allow visitors to experience the dolphins and sharks close-up. The park also has research and rehabilitation facilities for marine animals and 'behind-the-scenes' tours can be arranged.

The southern shores of KwaZulu-Natal are divided into two: the Sunshine Coast (from Amanzimtoti, near Durban, down to Mtwalume) and the Hibiscus Coast (from Hibberdene to Port Edward), also dubbed the 'Golf Coast' because of its many superb courses.

The shoreline that extends away to the north of Durban, from Umhlanga Rocks to the Tugela River Mouth, is called the Dolphin Coast, an inviting 90-km stretch of secluded coves and rock pools that beckon to those who prefer the smaller, more intimate kind of resort. The dolphins for which it is named can often be seen riding the waves.

For those who want to know more about the Zulu nation, there's Shakaland, a unique tourist venue and cultural village that started off as the film set for the epic *Shaka Zulu*. This working museum of Zulu

▶ Durban's uShaka Marine World offers visitors the ultimate close encounter with marine life.

culture, customs and lifestyle features Zulu dancing, traditional dress, the rigorous formality of stick-fighting, the forging of assegais, the weaving of grass mats and baskets and the making of the great red-clay, fire-blackened, beer drinking pots. Visitor accommodation is in traditional grass huts, though modern conveniences have been skilfully incorporated. Traditional stews served with staples of putu and samp made from maize and beans can be tasted and, for the more adventurous, there is *utshwala*, the traditional millet beer, drunk from a communal clay pot.

On 24 September each year (Heritage Day), Zulus in the traditional warrior garb – plumes and feathered anklets, patterned oxhide shield and the short, lethal stabbing spear that once struck terror into the hearts of thousands – gather at a small white marble monument in the north coast town of KwaDukuza (Stanger) to commemorate the death of Shaka, the ruthless and brilliant creator of the Zulu nation and one of Africa's greatest leaders.

The land that lies to the north of the Tugela River is subtropically lush, ecologically varied, and parts of it are a splendid refuge for the wild animals of Africa, some of them severely threatened elsewhere.

Hluhluwe-Imfolozi Park is a 96 000-ha area that boasts more than 80 mammal and 400 bird species. The Hluhluwe section lies in moist, hilly country while the Imfolozi section is on lower ground, with vegetation that is drier and starker and where flat-topped thorn trees dot the grasslands. The park is renowned for its rhino conservation efforts, but other wildlife includes elephant, lion, buffalo, cheetah, leopard, wildebeest, giraffe and a variety of antelope.

Mkhuze is a 40 000-ha haven that forms part of the iSimangaliso (Greater St Lucia) Wetland Park and lies at the southern edge of the Mozambique plain. The reserve is a favourite winter game-viewing destination, and well-placed hides provide excellent viewing points for birdwatchers.

The iSimangaliso (Greater St Lucia) Wetland Park is a World Heritage Site and extends over some 332 000 ha. It could be described as one of the most varied – and most beautiful – protected areas of its kind in the world. The giant, shallow, saline Lake St Lucia is the focal point, but the park also encompasses a massive spread of wetlands, estuaries, coastal forest, dune forest, mangrove swamps, African savanna and, in the adjoining marine reserve, coral reefs. This varied habitat sustains a remarkable diversity of animal, bird, fish and plant life.

There's much for the visitor to see and do within the iSimangaliso complex – hiking, fishing, game spotting, birdwatching, diving and wilderness trailing. Fishing and scuba diving are the main attractions among the beautiful offshore coral reefs.

Maputaland, at the far northern extremity of KwaZulu-Natal, lies between the Indian Ocean in the east and the Lebombo mountains in the west. This territory is a mix of evergreen woodland and savanna, dense forest, wetland,

floodplain, river estuary and the world's highest forested dunes, all of which are home to a wealth of animal, bird and plant life. Offshore are coral-encrusted reefs that entice scuba divers and marine biologists from across the world, while the sandy beaches play host to the threatened loggerhead and leatherback turtles, species that travel thousands of kilometres to nest along the same stretch of sand on which they were hatched.

In the extreme north of Maputaland is Tembe Elephant Park, a reserve designed to protect the remnants of the once great herds that, for thousands of years, wandered freely over the plain that stretches far into Mozambique. Although their numbers were drastically reduced as a result of both human settlement and warfare in neighbouring Mozambique, the elephant population is recovering and the park can lay claim to being home to the largest elephants in Africa. Just to the west, close to the Lebombo mountains, is Ndumu Game Reserve, regarded by some birdwatchers as having the highest concentration of birdlife in one area on the subcontinent.

For centuries the local Tembe people have used an intricate system of fish kraals in the lower reaches of the Kosi Estuary. The kraals, built with thick sticks embedded in the sandy bottom and interwoven with tree branches or rope fashioned from plant fibre, are spread out in spirals across the lower part of four connected lakes. As the tides come and go the fish migrate from the sea into the lake system and its confining kraals, where they are speared by the fishermen.

▶ Pietermaritzburg town hall is an excellent example of the town's colonial architecture.

▶ The city of Durban has a large Hindu population, descendants of indentured labourers from the nineteenth century, who celebrate Diwali, or the festival of lights, every year.

▶ The sun rises over Durban's Golden Mile (above), a 6-km stretch that lures sun-seekers to its golden beaches. At night (opposite) the Golden Mile offers a heady mix of entertainments, from hotels and restaurants to bars and clubs.

▶ Surfers flock to Durban's Golden Mile to enjoy the
near-perfect waves.

▶ The histories of KwaZulu-Natal and the Zulu kingdom are intricately interwoven. DumaZulu Cultural Village (above) and Shakaland allow visitors to experience traditional Zulu culture and learn more about these proud people. ▶ Ghostly fever trees, *Acacia xanthophloea* (overleaf), often line the waterways in Maputaland.

▶ Lake Sibaya (above) in the iSimangaliso (Greater St Lucia) Wetland Park is the largest freshwater lake in South Africa. ▶ The Tembe people of Maputaland (right) use an intricate system of fish kraals (fish traps) to catch fish in the Kosi Estuary.

Frontier Country

▶ Shark Rock Pier in Port Elizabeth.

The Wild Coast and Eastern Cape

The Eastern Cape stretches along the Indian Ocean coastline from beyond Cape St Francis in the west to the KwaZulu-Natal border, and inland to the semi-arid plains of the Great Karoo and, to the northeast, the foothills of the Drakensberg.

The mountains of the Eastern Cape are rounder, greener, less jaggedly rugged than those of its western neighbour, and they lie farther inland, making room for a broader coastal plain. The many perennial rivers of the hinterland cut deep gorges as they snake their way to the sea. Further north, between the coastal rampart and a second series of mountain ranges, is the plain of the Little Karoo, a gentler, better watered, far more productive land than its big brother, the Great Karoo, in the country's vast interior. The coastline, especially that toward the east, is famed for its wild beauty.

The region is traditional Xhosa country and the birthplace of Nelson Mandela, Steve Biko and many other heroes of the liberation struggle. It is also the cradle of English-speaking South Africa. The British settlers landed at Algoa Bay (now Port Elizabeth) in 1820, and the contribution they and their descendants made to the country's social and cultural fabric is preserved in the little city of Grahamstown.

The Transkei region runs from the Mthamvuna River on the KwaZulu-Natal border to the Great Kei River to the south-east, a beautiful 280-km stretch laced by lagoons, estuaries and sandy bays. It is a hiker's and holiday-maker's paradise. But, for all its beauty and seeming tranquillity, this is the Wild Coast: from the earliest days of maritime travel, ships have been driven shoreward by the treacherous currents and winds, to be smashed and swallowed by rocks and sea.

A modern explorer, though, can walk the coastline in just 25 days. The route is completed in easy stages, hikers overnighting in hospitable huts – a far cry from the anguish suffered by the survivors of the shipwrecked *Grosvenor*. The ship foundered near the mouth of the Mzimvubu River and, of its 135 survivors who

set out on the formidable journey to Algoa Bay, only six men arrived to tell the tale. Today the route traverses some of South Africa's most spectacular scenery, a mix of golden beaches, mangrove swamps, broad estuaries, waterfalls and massive cliffs. The only man-made interruptions – apart from a few hotels and casinos – are the tiny coastal settlements, isolated trading stores and thatched mud huts of the Xhosa. Although western styles have largely supplanted tribal dress and customs, these traditional brown-and-white structures have endured, their white sides confronting the sun to deflect the midday heat, their unpainted ones facing west to absorb the late afternoon warmth and conserve it for the night.

The start of the annual Sardine Run, often called 'the greatest shoal on earth', takes place in June or July in the waters off the Wild Coast. The enormous shoals of sardines, often kilometres long, start far out at sea in the cold waters off the southern Cape and begin to make their way up the east coast of the African continent. Sharks, sea birds, big game fish and dolphins follow the run in a spectacular procession all the way up to KwaZulu-Natal. The run continues for about a week, and is then gone as suddenly and mysteriously as it appeared.

Between Port Edward and Port St Johns two dramatic sculptures have been gouged from the rocks by the perpetual pounding of the sea – Cathedral Rock and the Castle. To the south is the dramatic dolerite intrusion of Brazen Head and the splendid evergreen forests and prolific waterfowl of Hluleka Reserve. Beyond Coffee Bay, a black pebble beach lies alongside Hole-in-the-Wall, a massive, detached sandstone cliff through which the sea has eroded a perfect archway. There is a perpetual, thunderous roar as the water rushes through the opening, which has earned it the appropriate Xhosa name *esiKhaleni* – the place of sound.

The Xhosa believe that preparation for life is a matter of example and of ritual: a man's success depends on how he lives and how he respects tribal lore, taboos and customs. Boys attend *Khwetha*, or circumcision school, which is the ritual transition to manhood and preparation for marriage. *Khwetha* involves a three-month period of strict seclusion, during which the young men live together, their identities concealed behind white sandstone paint smeared from head to toe – both a symbol of purity and a defence against evil. After the initiation period, the ritual burning of the hut used during the seclusion denotes the end of boyhood.

The Great Kei River, on its way to the warm Indian Ocean, has cut gorges so deep that they form a prominent boundary, a line that divides the land into 'beyond the Kei' and 'this side of the Kei'. This is a region of surprising contrasts, where affluence rubs shoulders with soul-destroying poverty and casinos, and luxurious marine resorts are the near neighbours of dwellings made of mud and reed. But it is for the beauty of the coastline that this region is best known. Separating the pockets of development is a string of beaches etched with estuaries, dunes and coastal forests, which provide an undisturbed and beautiful habitat for birds and other wild creatures. The five-day Strandloper Trail is one of a number of hikes that explore this section of the coast.

The region is also the birthplace of Nelson Mandela, and those interested in finding out about the history surrounding this great leader can explore the Nelson Mandela Route. The route starts in King William's Town and includes a visit to the grave of Steve Biko, the leader of the Black Consciousness movement, then moves

▶ Crafts and curios for sale along the roadside.

onto Bhisho and Mthatha, the first location of the Nelson Mandela Museum. Other sections of the museum are in Qunu, the village where he spent his childhood, and Mveso, where he was born. The route ends in the city of East London at the city's museum.

The coelacanth, which was thought by scientists to have been extinct for more than 70 million years, was rediscovered when a live specimen was caught near East London in 1938. The discovery caused an international sensation and brought world renown to Prof. JLB Smith, the man who identified it. The coelacanth became known as 'old fourlegs' from Smith's reference to its unusual arrangement of fins. The original South African specimen is housed at the East London Museum. It's worth noting that the world's only dodo egg is also an exhibit at this institution.

Inland of East London are the lofty peaks of the Amatola mountains, known to the Xhosa as 'the little cows', of which the Hogsback is a prominent part. The mountains are often snow-capped in winter, wreathed in cool mists in summer, and they rise above the slopes and foothills of a scenically stunning region.

The mountain slopes are densely forested with indigenous sneezewood, ironwood and yellowwood trees, and everywhere there are spectacular waterfalls, dappled trout streams and cold, clear pools. Among the peaks and valleys is a line of three arched ridges, the one known as First Hogsback most closely resembling the back of a sturdy pig. Hogsback and its forests and falls should be explored on foot along the well-planned paths where rest stops are usually outstanding view sites. This is a quiet country, one that seems to offer the ultimate in solitude, but it is also home to Amatola toads and Hogsback frogs, giant golden moles, earthworms up to 3 m long, Samango monkeys, and the rare blue duiker.

The small church of St Patrick's-on-the-hill and the Eco-shrine overlooking the Tyume gorge are worth a visit. For visitors with an interest in history, the area around Hogsback is also dotted with the ruins of forts that were built by the British during the colonial wars against the dispossessed Xhosa.

Port Elizabeth, often called 'the friendly city', is situated to the south and offers an extraordinary diversity of attractions as well as its legendary friendliness. It's an ideal location from which to explore not only the endless beaches but also some fascinating natural and social history, the orchards of the hinterland and the small towns and remote landscapes of the central and eastern Great Karoo.

The Donkin Heritage Trail through the city centre, which links 47 places of interest, shows off some of Port Elizabeth's intriguing nineteenth-century architecture. Also included on the trail is the 51.8-m-high Campanile, which commemorates the landing of the 1820 Settlers. Bayworld, which is made up of the Oceanarium, Port Elizabeth Museum and Snake Park, is a popular tourist attraction. Dolphins, seals and penguins can be viewed at the Oceanarium and a variety of snakes and reptiles are housed at the Snake Park. The Museum carries both cultural and natural history exhibits and also features a hall of maritime history.

Grahamstown, to the east of Port Elizabeth, plays host to the annual National Arts Festival, which takes place during winter. The small city is the home of Rhodes University and the festival came about to celebrate and promote the English language. Today, however, it embraces all the languages of South Africa and represents all art forms, from craft art and jazz to street and children's theatre.

The Addo Elephant National Park lies in the valley of the Sundays River at the foot of the Zuurberg mountains. It is home to black rhino, Cape buffalo, eland, kudu, red hartebeest and other varieties of antelope, as well as to 170 bird species, among them hawks, finches and moorhens. The flightless dung beetle, restricted almost exclusively to the park, is also found here. The park was proclaimed in 1931 to protect the 11 remaining elephants in the area. It has since expanded to 164 000 ha and its elephant population has grown to around 450. Future plans for the park include expansion to 360 000 ha, a large portion of which will come from the incorporation of the marine reserve currently under the park's protection. The world's largest breeding colony of Cape gannets and second largest colony of African penguins are on the islands in this reserve. This will also mean that Addo will become the first Big Seven reserve, where visitors stand the chance of seeing lion, leopard, rhino, elephant, buffalo, whales and great white sharks.

▶ The Cathedral of St Michael and St George, Grahamstown.

▶ The Hole-in-the-Wall (left) near Coffee Bay on the Wild Coast is also known as *esiKhaleni*, or 'the place of sound', because of the roar of the waves as they rush through the gap in the rock. ▶ Many areas of the Wild Coast are still rural, and traditional homesteads (above) are dotted across the coastal cliffs. ▶ The Amadiba Horse Trail (overleaf) along the Wild Coast is a great way to see the more remote areas of the Eastern Cape.

▶ The Wild Coast is a region of secluded beaches and exquisite natural beauty – the ideal destination for those who want to get away from it all.

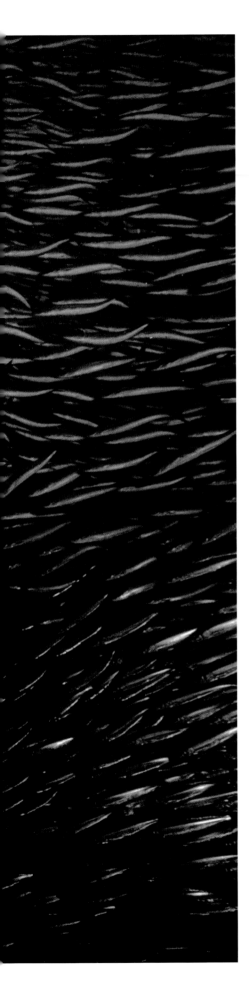

▶ The annual phenomenon of the Sardine Run (left), or 'the greatest shoal on earth', begins its journey somewhere off the Wild Coast. The spectacle continues northwards up the coast to KwaZulu-Natal before vanishing as quickly as it started. ▶ The Oceanarium at Bayworld in Port Elizabeth is a popular attraction where visitors can experience dolphins close-up (above). A museum and snake park also form part of the Bayworld educational and conservation complex.

▶ The flightless dung beetle (top) is found almost exclusively in the Addo Elephant National Park, while the fiscal flycatcher (above) is just one of about 170 bird species to be found here. ▶ Although elephants (right and overleaf) are the main drawcard at Addo, the park is the first in South Africa to be declared home of the Big Seven – elephant, buffalo, rhino, lion, leopard, whale and great white shark.

The Garden Route

South Africa's enchanting coastal Eden

The Cape south coast's 'garden' stretches from Heidelberg in the west to Storms River in the east, a scenically stunning region which is superbly developed for tourism. This area is renowned for its natural beauty, beautiful beaches and indigenous forests and there is much to see and do. A number of reserves and a national park offer visitors the chance to experience the animal and birdlife of the region in their natural habitat, and three of South Africa's top hiking trails, namely the Otter, Dolphin and Tsitsikamma, are also found here.

The Garden Route has long been a favourite of both local and foreign tourists and, especially during the summer months, the area is a popular holiday destination. Swimming, fishing and boating are a few of the aquatic activities on offer and the wide range of accommodation often means that visitors are spoilt for choice.

A premier attraction of the region is the Garden Route National Park, which protects more than 157 000 ha of forest and fynbos between Wilderness in the west and Oubosstrand in the east. Proclaimed in 2009, it combines the former Wilderness and Tsitsikamma national parks and the Knysna Lakes Area, as well as vast tracts of indigenous state forests and provincial nature reserves. Its rest camps, chalets and camping grounds at Wilderness, Storms River Mouth, Nature's Valley, Harkerville forest and Diepwalle, north of Knysna, are particularly popular during the school holidays.

Plettenberg Bay, affectionately known as Plett, is a beautiful resort which lies beside lagoons and river mouths at the eastern end of the Garden Route. Plettenberg Bay and its surrounds are spectacularly beautiful; the area is blessed with 320 days of virtually uninterrupted sunshine a year; its clear warm waters, safe swimming and fine white sands are incomparable. It is also here that you'll find the exquisite pansy shell, symbol of Plettenberg Bay and a holiday souvenir that will outrank all others.

Flanking the fine resort hotel on Beacon Island are two of the three major swimming beaches, Central and Robberg. The former is quite literally on the hotel's front doorstep and is favoured by families; the latter is a long curve of golden sand ending in a rocky punctuation at the Robberg Peninsula, a nature and marine reserve endowed with rich bird and intertidal life. The reserve also embraces an important archaeological site, Nelson Bay Cave, once occupied by the Khoekhoe and the San. A fairly well-preserved child's skeleton, dating from about 700 BCE has been found in one of three Robberg burial sites that have also yielded a wealth of shells, stone artefacts and ostrich eggshell beads.

To the east of Plettenberg Bay are the Lookout Rocks, from where you can observe the giant southern right whales that come inshore to mate during the winter months. Beyond is Bietou Lagoon, a paradise for the water-skier and yachting enthusiast.

The Otter Trail, South Africa's first organised hiking trail, is still one of the country's most popular. It follows the rock-bound and scenically superb coast from Storms River Mouth to the lovely village and reserve of Nature's Valley. Walkers take five days to cover the 42.5-km route. The terrain can be tough and includes traversing sections of the Tsitsikamma forest and crossing – by swimming or wading – the mouth of the Bloukrans River.

Knysna's tidal lagoon is one of the largest South African estuaries. Its diverse habitats are home to many species of birds and fish, the country's largest oyster-farming centre and the rare Knysna sea horse.

The waters of the lagoon are an artist's delight and a holiday-maker's paradise. The imposing sandstone cliffs that flank the lagoon's entrance were once feared by mariners who had to negotiate the sand bar between them, but today The Heads are a tourist drawcard and the lagoon is home to the local yacht squadron, houseboats for hire, myriad small leisure craft and a few pleasure cruisers that carry visitors across the waters to the western headland and the private Featherbed Nature Reserve.

The central part of Knysna is on the north shore, with numerous pubs and restaurants and an immense range of accommodation for tourists. Thesen's Island, once the base of the region's timber industry, is now a residential and commercial centre and home of the well-known Knysna Oyster Company. The Knysna Oyster Festival takes place every year during winter – usually July – and thousands take part in celebrating and tasting the area's best-known delicacy. Another annual

▶ The spectacularly colourful Knysna turaco.

event in the town is the Pink Loerie Mardi Gras, which takes place in April and is a highlight on the international gay calendar.

The little stone church of the Holy Trinity in Belvidere was built in the mid-nineteenth century and is a faithful copy of an early Norman church. Wood used in the building was cut in the forests that still surround the town and extend for almost 200 km along the Outeniqua and Tsitsikamma mountain slopes. The region's trees, on which the early economy of Knysna depended almost exclusively, include ironwood, white alder, stinkwood and yellowwood.

There are also huge plantations of introduced species such as pine and eucalyptus, but it is the indigenous forest that fascinates the nature lover. Leopards and vervet monkeys, wild pigs and several species of small antelope are among the numerous creatures that live here. Birdlife, too, is prolific, and this is the preferred habitat of the vividly coloured and crested Knysna turaco.

To the west of Knysna lies the Wilderness resort and its beautiful lagoon at the mouth of the Touw River. This is a favourite place for holidays and honeymoons. Children love the shallow shores of the lagoon, while the deeper channels provide an ideal venue for watersports. Surfers favour nearby Victoria Bay, which also offers the best bathing in the area.

There are five major lakes to the east of Wilderness, all saltwater and linked to the sea with the exception of the most easterly one. This is freshwater Groenvlei or Lake Pleasant and, like the other lakes, including Wilderness lagoon, it owes its creation to some complicated geomorphological sequences. The Lakes Area of the Garden Route National Park, between Knysna and Wilderness, is rich in birdlife and is a favourite spot for nature lovers. There are also numerous hikes and trails in the area.

The Little Karoo lies inland from the Garden Route. The climate of this semi-arid region, of which Oudtshoorn is the unofficial capital, is ideally suited to the ostrich. The town, set against the backdrop of the Swartberg Mountains, began life modestly enough, but when ostrich feathers became accessories of high fashion from the 1860s, the 50-year boom that followed made Oudtshoorn one of the busiest and most prosperous towns of the old Cape Colony.

'Feather barons' built 'feather palaces' – lavish, ornate, romantic monuments to the staggering wealth of the early 1900s. The vast Edwardian mansion of Pinehurst, designed by the Dutch-born architect Johannes Vixseboxse, is but one such example. Vixseboxse was among the many professionals, artisans, adventurers and entrepreneurs who flocked to Oudtshoorn during its boom era. The CP Nel Museum's exhibits showcase the heritage of the town and the region of the Little Karoo, and the synagogue is acknowledgement of the contribution made by the Jewish community.

But Oudtshoorn is not all about ostriches and architecture. The annual Klein Karoo National Arts Festival (KKNK), which celebrates Afrikaans arts and culture, attracts thousands of visitors to the town each year. The festival programme includes music, drama, art and film and features some of South Africa's top talent.

And within the Swartberg Mountains to the north of Oudtshoorn is the world's most extensive system of limestone caverns, known as the Cango Caves. Discoveries of tools near the cave mouth have proved that the caves were known to humans as far back as 80 000 years. Massive, ancient stalactites and stalagmites extend from the caverns' roofs and floors, as well as other, more recent formations: the intricately curled helictites, for example, only a few centuries old, or the great sheets of dripstone that defy any assessment of age. Guided tours into the caves with accredited guides take place several times every day.

▶ The Otter Trail is one of South Africa's most popular hikes.

▶ A picturesque ravine in the Storms River area of the Garden Route (above). ▶ Robberg Peninsula (right), a marine and nature reserve, extends about four kilometres into the sea and offers visitors spectacular ocean views. There are several hiking routes to choose from as well as scores of picnic spots.

▶ The Knysna Heads (left and above) are a well-known feature of the area. The eastern head is known for its upmarket holiday homes and guest houses, while the private Featherbed Nature Reserve dominates the western head. ▶ The Knysna lagoon (top) is home to the rare and endangered Knysna sea horse.

▶ Oudtshoorn in the Little Karoo (above) became famous across the world during the feather boom of the late nineteenth century. Today, ostriches (opposite) are still an important part of the local economy, but are now bred more for their meat than their feathers. ▶ The Cango Caves (overleaf) just outside Oudtshoorn make up the world's most extensive system of limestone caverns.

▶ Although it appears desolate, the |Ai-|Ais/Richtersveld Transfrontier National Park is actually teeming with life and is rich in desert flora.

Flowering deserts and landscapes that stretch forever

The vast, dry upland plateau that makes up the greater part of the South African interior might hold little attraction for most travellers, but there are those who are captivated by the clarity of the air, the stillness and the freedom of its boundless spaces. South Africa's central plateau covers almost 400 000 km², about one-third of the whole of South Africa.

This is the Karoo, a seemingly endless area dominated by Karoo veld, a vegetation adapted to survive drought, extremes of heat and cold, and intense sunshine. Surprisingly nourishing, this scrubby vegetation sustains flocks of Merino sheep, imparting a tenderness and herby flavour that has made Karoo mutton a delicacy.

Roughly divided into the Little and Great Karoo, the plateau is deprived of coastal rains by the Cape Fold mountains along its southern and south-western rim. Water is the Karoo's most precious asset and windmills punctuate the plains, drawing the moisture from beneath the ground and pumping it to remote farms and grazing outposts. The tiny towns of the Karoo lie far apart, many dating back to the mid-1700s when farms were established, prospered, and attracted other settlers to the remote interior. Many of the towns, such as Graaff-Reinet, have been declared areas of historic interest and are thus protected. In these towns, open water furrows line the streets, taking *leiwater* into backyards and gardens. The system allows even the smallest village garden to produce a generous harvest of sweet, sun-ripened fruit and a profusion of roses.

But under the sun-seared surface lies another bounty, rich fossil remains that provide an almost unbroken record of 50 million years of evolution and which draw palaeontologists, geologists and botanists to the region.

To the casual observer the Karoo may be nothing more than a barren plateau with a harsh climate. But it inspired Jacob Pierneef to paint, Olive Schreiner and Sir Laurens van der Post to write, and Helen Martins to create the Owl House in Nieu Bethesda, just four among the many who have been seduced by this region.

The Little and Great Karoo are separated from the coastal strip and from each other by a series of mountain ranges. Nearest the coast, and forming the southern boundary of the Little Karoo, are the Langeberg and Outeniqua mountains. Further inland are the Klein and Groot Swartberg ranges, towering barriers between the Little Karoo and the vast, dry central plateau of the Great Karoo.

The Swartberg Pass between Oudtshoorn and Prince Albert is a 30-km engineering marvel of sheer drops and hairpin bends, which climbs to 1 615 m above sea level. Travel over the pass is inadvisable in bad weather, or for anyone with a less-than-reliable vehicle and a bad head for heights. But the views are panoramic and can be enjoyed from vantage sites and picnic spots along the way.

Meiringspoort was the first link between the Little and Great Karoo and it weaves between cliff faces with almost vertical contortions in the Table Mountain sandstone strata. The mountain unfolds in a continually surprising series of vistas, each more dramatic than the last.

To visit the spectacular Augrabies Falls, it is usual to join the Orange River at Upington and follow its course through Keimoes and Kakamas to the Augrabies Falls National Park. Upington revolves around the rich harvests of fruit cultivated on the irrigated, fertile banks of the river. In stark contrast, however, are the town's northern landscapes of red Kalahari dunes.

Further west, the little town of Keimoes has a working Victorian waterwheel and a tiny historic mission church, both of which can be seen along the Main Road. Tierberg Nature Reserve, a haven for springbok and winter-flowering aloes, is just outside the town. From the lookout, there is a panoramic view across the Orange River Valley.

Kakamas is located in one of the most fertile areas of the lower Orange River Valley. Apart from its massive hydroelectric power station, the town's long-standing relationship with the river can be seen in the canals, waterwheels and irrigation tunnels built by immigrant Cornish miners.

Augrabies Falls National Park has a rich variety of birdlife, mammals and drought-resistant flora. But it is the spectacular Augrabies Falls that bring visitors here, to the 'place of great noise', as the

▶ The Valley of Desolation lies near the historical town of Graaff-Reinet.

Nama people called it. The Orange River seems to gather speed as it approaches the narrow channels along the gorge and is released in torrents of white water, plummeting into the ravine below, roaring like thunder as it goes.

One of the most pleasant ways of exploring the park is to do the three-day Klipspringer hiking trail. Other options include the shorter Dassie nature trail or the Gariep 3-in-1 Adventure, which includes a 3-km canoe trip on the Orange River, a 4-km walk and an 11-km mountain bike ride.

In the extreme northern corner of South Africa lies the Kgalagadi Transfrontier Park, the first transfrontier park in Africa and a joint partnership between South Africa and Botswana. It is one of the world's largest conservation areas and, with no dividing fences, the animals are able to migrate freely between the two territories. Most numerous are springbok and gemsbok, followed by wildebeest, red hartebeest and eland. The black-maned Kalahari lion is king of the park's predator population, which includes leopard, cheetah, black-backed jackal, bat-eared fox, brown and spotted hyaena, suricate, African wild cat, caracal and mongoose.

The Kalahari's duneland, the largest continuous stretch of sand in the world, is seen at its most striking from the air, with vast reaches of wave-like ripples in an ocean of red sand reaching from the equator to the Orange River, and from Angola to Zimbabwe. The only punctuation is given by bleached riverbeds with their windmills, watering holes and camel thorn trees, and the scattered patches of the salt pans which gave the Kalahari its name – derived from *kgalagadi* in the San language, it means 'place of thirst'.

There is no perennial water in the park – the Auob flows perhaps once every five years, the Nossob once every fifty. The rain comes sporadically, usually as a thunderstorm. More often, the skies are clear and this causes temperatures to rocket to 40 °C in summer and drop to a freezing –10 °C on winter nights.

The dunes, riverbeds and plains of the Kalahari support shrub savanna vegetation interspersed with scattered trees, providing the animals with a surprisingly reliable and nutritious diet. One of the most common Kalahari trees is the shepherd's tree or 'tree of life', *Boscia albitrunca*, which provides year-round fodder. The tsamma melon and gemsbok cucumber provide both food and a vital source of moisture to the birds and animals of the region.

The far-western Namaqualand region is characterised by immense stretches of semi-arid, thinly vegetated plain punctuated by granite outcrops. The land stretches from the Orange River south to Doringbaai and includes about 1 000 km of coastline, backed by a narrow strip of red and white sand known as the Sandveld, often mantled by a dense mist. In a region of searing summer temperatures and erratic annual rainfall, this mist is life-sustaining for an enormous variety of plants.

For the greater part of the year the seeds of a million plants and flowers lie dormant – until the first rains. Then, almost instantaneously, they push through the earth and the wilderness is flooded with lakes of colour. This spectacle is at its best from mid-August to late September, and even October if the rains are late.

Many Cape country towns – Clanwilliam, Calvinia, Darling, Nieuwoudtville, Tulbagh, Caledon – have superb shows of spring flowers, but the drive from Cape Town 550 km up the West Coast to Springbok and beyond takes in the finest flower country and some fascinating towns to boot.

North of Springbok and bordering Namibia is the |Ai-|Ais/Richtersveld Transfrontier National Park. The park is jointly managed by the Nama people and South African National Parks and was declared a UNESCO World Heritage Site in 2007. This is vast, stark and silent countryside with extraordinary lunar landscapes and unnerving plant adaptations such as the *halfmens* trees, which resemble people, and usually face north, towards the sun.

The West Coast has a remote and haunting beauty which, once seen, can never be forgotten. The true West Coast starts immediately west of Agulhas, the southernmost tip of Africa, but colloquially, the West Coast is the seaboard running northwards from Melkbosstrand to the border of the Northern Cape, as well as the inland towns from Darling north to Clanwilliam and the Cederberg area. The wealth and variety of its birdlife, wild flowers and excellent seafood bring seasonal visitors from north and south during the spring and early summer months.

Taking pride of place in a region boasting extensive sanctuaries for marine and terrestrial flora and fauna is the West Coast National Park. Langebaan Lagoon, a significant wetland area and one of the world's more important bird sanctuaries, forms part of the park. Invertebrates provide a rich diet for the turnstones, sanderlings and other migrant waders, while summer brings tens of thousands of Arctic visitors, including curlew sandpipers. Several islands in the lagoon support resident species – blackbacked gulls, cormorants, African penguins and a large population of African black oystercatchers.

▶ During spring the semi-desert landscape of Namaqualand is transformed.

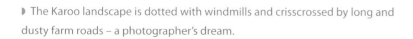
The Karoo landscape is dotted with windmills and crisscrossed by long and dusty farm roads – a photographer's dream.

The Karoo is a place of tranquillity, solitude and the occasional farmstead. Many farms and small Karoo towns offer overnight accommodation for city slickers wanting to experience the remoteness of this region. The magnificent Augrabies Falls in full flow (overleaf). The falls get their name from the Nama people, who called this the 'place of great noise'.

▶ The Richtersveld is a treasure-trove of desert flora and fauna (left). ▶ The tracks of a gemsbok trace a line across a characteristic red dune of the Kalahari (above).

▶ Despite being known as 'the place of thirst', the Kgalagadi Transfrontier Park supports an abundance of wildlife, from playful meerkats (left) to the famous black-maned lions (above) of the Kalahari.

◗ During the driest months of the year the afternoon winds kick up dust storms across the Kgalagadi (left). Yet even in these desperate times the tsamma melon (above) provides life-giving moisture to the region's animals and birds.

▶ Table Mountain is synonymous with the spirit of Cape Town and South Africa. The Khoekhoen called it *Hoerikwaggo*, or 'sea mountain'.

Mountains, vineyards and shipwrecks

Table Mountain, the 350 million-year-old massif of sandstone and shale, is an extraordinary natural feature and is synonymous with the spirit of Cape Town. The Khoekhoen called it *Hoerikwaggo*, which means 'sea mountain', and when they lived here around 4 000 years ago, the lower slopes glittered with huge groves of indigenous silver trees. Table Mountain today forms part of the Table Mountain National Park, which stretches from Signal Hill all the way to Cape Point in the south. The Cape Floristic Region also forms part of the park, and with around 8 200 plant species it is the smallest and richest of the six floral kingdoms on earth, and as such has been declared a Natural World Heritage Site.

Other areas that form part of the park include the Cape of Good Hope and Cape Point, Boulders African penguin colony near Simon's Town, the beautiful fynbos landscape of Silvermine, and the Afromontane forests.

Cape Town, the once tiny 'Tavern of the Seas', so named for its early tradition of hospitality to seafarers, is today a vibrant international city. The V&A Waterfront development is much more than a great tourist drawcard, it has helped restore the city's links with the sea. What distinguishes the V&A Waterfront from similar developments around the world is that it is the only working leisure port where traditional harbour activities take place alongside quayside entertainments. The main area focuses on leisure, with a range of hotels, restaurants and shopping facilities, while the Two Oceans Aquarium is a must-see for any visitor, especially for families. The aquarium showcases the marine diversity of the Atlantic and Indian oceans and is home to over 3 000 marine animals. There is also Nobel Square, erected as a tribute to South Africa's Nobel Peace Prize laureates.

The Nelson Mandela Gateway is the departure point for the daily ferries to Robben Island. The island, situated 12 km off Cape Town in Table Bay, was used over the centuries as a leper colony and a hospital for the mentally ill, but it is its use as a maximum security prison for political prisoners that gave the island world recognition. Today it is a popular tourist attraction and World Heritage Site, and serves as a symbol of the triumph of the human spirit over hardship and adversity.

Cape Town is renowned for the architectural beauty of its oldest buildings, among them the pentagonal Castle of Good Hope, St George's Cathedral, the Slave Lodge Museum, and many of the restored Victorian shops in Long Street. Also worth a visit is the Company's Garden, which was created by Jan van Riebeeck to supply fresh produce to passing ships.

The Bo-Kaap (upper Cape Town) is the heart of the city's Muslim population. There is a strong sense of community in this district; the cobbled streets, the picturesque, pastel-painted houses, and the cries of the *bilal* summoning the faithful to prayer are typical everyday images.

The Cape Peninsula features about 150 km of scenic coastline sculpted into myriad bays and beaches. The coastal drive from the city meanders along the beachfront to Sea Point, then Clifton and Camps Bay, and on to Bakoven, where the drive opens up to an unspoilt coastline of extraordinary beauty. Over the nek the road reveals Hout Bay lying below, with its fishing-village atmosphere and beautiful bay. The spectacular Chapman's Peak Drive starts at Hout Bay and continues past Noordhoek's Long Beach, hangout of surfers and horseriders.

The massively imposing promontory of Cape Point constitutes the southern boundary of the Cape of Good Hope reserve, which forms part of the Table Mountain National Park. The reserve is rich in floral diversity, particularly fynbos, and in September and October the spring flowers are a delight. Reptiles such as snakes and tortoises live among the shrubbery, and the rare Cape platanna is safeguarded in this protected habitat. Antelope and mountain zebra also live here, as well as chacma baboon. Nearly 250 species of land- and seabirds have been recorded here, ranging from cormorants to minuscule sunbirds. A lookout site at the very tip of Cape Point, perched on the highest sea cliffs in the country, offers unforgettable views of the turbulent sea far below. Walking trails and hikes are a great way to see the park, and whale-watching points and viewsites are well signposted.

Simon's Town is a blend of Victorian seaside village and bustling naval base, and is steeped in

▶ Long Street in Cape Town is the city's favourite spot for night-time entertainment.

naval history. For many of the visitors who come to Simon's Town, however, history is the last thing on their minds as they head for its glorious beaches. The town's proximity to Boulders beach and its resident African penguins, as well as the Cape of Good Hope, makes it a popular holiday destination in the summer months.

The Cape Peninsula's southern suburbs were once a string of villages sprawled along the foothills of Table Mountain. Several display legacies of one of the Cape's most influential men, Cecil John Rhodes, and most prominent of these is Rhodes Memorial on the slopes of Devil's Peak. Overlooked by Rhodes Memorial are some of the ivy-covered sandstone buildings of the upper campus of the University of Cape Town, part of the country's oldest university. Further on lies the Groote Schuur manor house, the official residence to South African heads of state.

To the east is Wynberg, and its Chelsea area of exquisitely preserved and restored Cape vernacular and Victorian buildings. Another attraction of this charming suburb is Maynardville, a public park where a colourful charity community carnival takes place every year. There is also an open-air theatre where Shakespearean productions are staged in the summer.

Kirstenbosch National Botanical Garden is enjoyed by people from all over the world. Covering the eastern side of Table Mountain from the lower slopes to Maclear's Beacon, it extends over an area of 528 ha. The best known of South Africa's eight national botanical gardens, it was the first in the world to showcase only indigenous plants. There is also a comprehensive botanical library, a visitor's centre and a spacious conservatory displaying plants from arid and alpine areas. Kirstenbosch also serves as a concert venue during the summer months, and the annual Carols by Candlelight is popular over the Christmas period.

The grandest and oldest of the Cape's wine estates, Groot Constantia, lies no more than a 20-minute drive from the heart of Cape Town. The original estate was divided into three independent wine-producing farms: Groot Constantia, Klein Constantia and Buitenverwachting, and today each has a magnificent Cape Dutch homestead and produces a distinctive cellar of exclusive world-renowned wines.

When Simon van der Stel, in the late seventeenth century, instructed the newly settled burghers to plant vines in the Eerste River Valley, he laid the foundations for an industry which has brought world renown to all of South Africa. Stellenbosch is one of the most beautifully preserved towns in the country, with magnificent examples of Cape Dutch architecture, and it lies at the heart of a region that features over 200 cellars. The Stellenbosch wine route, South Africa's first, was established in 1971 and now includes more than 100 cellars, most of which are open to the public. Other key wine areas include Paarl, Franschhoek, Tulbagh, Worcester, Robertson and the Breede River Valley.

The wine-growing regions of the Cape span a wide area and the region has a number of micro-climates and contrasting growth environments, making it ideal for the production of both red and white wines from the very best grape varieties. Vineyards thrive in the cool coastal regions of the south-west Cape; in the blazing, dry heat of the Little Karoo interior; up the West Coast and across the Swartland; at Piketberg in the Sandveld and along the banks of the Olifants River. Scenic routes meander through most of the winelands, and excellent accommodation is available in all these districts.

The coastal town of Hermanus draws its visitors from all over the world and among the most regular of callers are the mighty whales. It may be as early in the year as May or June that the whale crier sounds his kelp horn to announce that the whales have returned. Walker Bay is one of the world's prime whale-spotting sites, and the best for land-based whale-watching. Southern right and humpback whales come in close to court and to mate, to calve and to raise their young.

To the south of Hermanus lies Cape Agulhas, the southernmost tip of Africa. The lighthouse at Agulhas is the second oldest in operation in South Africa, and this as well as the region surrounding it form part of the Agulhas National Park. Stone tidal fish traps, shell middens and pottery left behind by Khoisan hunter-gatherers are important cultural links to the past.

The De Hoop Nature Reserve, east of Bredasdorp, includes a marine section to conserve part of the Agulhas Bank, the richest fishing grounds in the southern hemisphere. The reserve also protects one of the largest remaining areas of coastal fynbos in the south-western Cape and is renowned for its birdlife.

▶ The entrance to the world-renowned Mount Nelson Hotel.

▶ The view at night over Cape Town, Table Bay and Lion's Head from the summit of Table Mountain. ▶ Robben Island (overleaf), once a maximum security prison for political prisoners, most notably Nelson Mandela, is today a UNESCO World Heritage Site.

▸ Cape Point and the Cape of Good Hope Reserve (previous spread) form part of the Table Mountain National Park and are among the region's prime tourist attractions. ▸ The V&A Waterfront development (above) is the top tourist destination in the city of Cape Town. ▸ Cape Town's colonial heritage is reflected in the architectural styles of some of its oldest buildings (opposite).

◗ Some of the colourfully painted houses of the Bo-Kaap, or upper Cape Town, have been in the same family for generations. This mainly Muslim community was originally established shortly after the abolition of slavery in the mid-nineteenth century.

▶ Clifton (left) is known as the playground of the wealthy and its exquisite beaches are the place to be seen in summer. ▶ The Sentinel, a peak at the end of the Karbonkelberg, stands guard over the entrance to Hout Bay harbour (above). ▶ The waters off Muizenberg (overleaf) are considerably warmer than those off the western coast of the peninsula, and are therefore popular with swimmers and surfers.

▶ Cape of Good Hope Reserve (left) and nearby Boulders Beach (top) are popular with both locals and tourists. Boulders, with its resident colony of African penguins, is especially popular for family outings. ▶ Kalk Bay (above), a picturesque harbour on the False Bay side of the peninsula, is where much of the superb linefish served in Cape restaurants is landed.

▶ Kirstenbosch National Botanical Garden is a sanctuary for about half of South Africa's enormous wealth of indigenous flowering species.

▶ There are five wine-growing regions in the Western Cape, all of which are crisscrossed by scenic wine routes. Franschhoek (left and above right) is where some producers still proudly uphold French wine-growing traditions. ▶ Buitenverwachting vines at dawn, Constantia (overleaf).

▶ Hermanus has the best land-based whale-watching in the world and visitors flock here during late winter and early spring to welcome the migrating whales (left). ▶ For those with a keen sense of adventure and the urge to get up close to a great white shark (above), cage diving near Gansbaai is a popular pastime.

▶ The lighthouse at Cape Agulhas (above) was built in 1849 and still warns ships of the treacherous Cape and its rocky seabed. ▶ The De Hoop Nature Reserve (opposite) near Bredasdorp includes a marine section to conserve part of the Agulhas Bank. It also protects the largest remaining areas of coastal fynbos in the south-western Cape.

GLOSSARY

Bushveld: Savanna; mainly refers to the hot, wild and uncultivated areas of northern South Africa.

Highveld: Refers to the inland plateau of South Africa, generally at an altitude of between 1 200 and 1 800 m above sea level.

Khoekhoe/Khoekhoen: Also Khoikhoi/Khoikhoin. The original inhabitants of the Cape, who were nomadic herders.

Khoisan: The collective term for the Khoekhoe and San peoples of southern Africa.

Kloof(s): A wooded valley or ravine.

Leiwater: An irrigation system, usually of open water furrows, which enables residents in Karoo towns to divert water onto their land for a specified period.

Lowveld: Refers to the subtropical region of north-eastern South Africa, namely Mpumalanga and Limpopo provinces, generally lying at an altitude of below 600 m above sea level.

Muti: Traditional medicine in South Africa, often prepared from herbs and parts of animals.

Nguni: A collective term for the Bantu-speaking peoples of southern Africa.

Poort: A narrow mountain pass.

San: The aboriginal people of southern Africa; also referred to as Bushmen.

Shebeen: An unlicensed establishment, sometimes a private house, that sells alcoholic drinks.

INDEX

Published by Struik Travel & Heritage
(an imprint of Penguin Random House (Pty) Ltd)
Company Reg. No. 1953/000441/07
The Estuaries No 4, Oxbow Crescent, Century Avenue, Century City, 7441
PO Box 1144, Cape Town 8000, South Africa

Get updates and news by subscribing to our monthly newsletter at
www.randomstruik.co.za

First published in 2008, Reprinted in 2009, 2010 (twice), 2012, 2013, 2015

10 9 8 7

ISBN: 978 1 77007 018 9

Publishing Manager: Claudia Dos Santos
Managing Editor: Roelien Theron
Project Coordinator: Alana Bolligelo
Additional text by Joy Clack and Denise Slabbert
Edited by Joy Clack and Roxanne Reid
Designed by Robin Cox
Picture research by Carmen Hartzenberg
Map by Desireé Oosterberg
Proofread by Mariëlle Renssen
Indexed by Joy Clack

Reproduction by Hirt & Carter Cape (Pty) Ltd
Printed and bound by Craft Print International Pte Ltd, Singapore

Front cover: Sunrise at Leisure Bay, South Coast, KwaZulu-Natal.
Back cover: Arch Rock in Featherbed Nature Reserve, Knysna, Garden Route.
Page 1: Rock pool near Kommetjie, Cape Town.
Page 2–3: Spring flowers in the Helderberg Nature Reserve near Cape Town.

Photographic credits

Adey, Shaen (IOA): pages 17 top left, 17 bottom left, 17 bottom right, 26–27, 53, 74, 79, 84–85, 86, 87, 88–89, 90, 91, 95 left, 102, 104, 109, 111 top, 119, 123 top, 146, 147, 148–149, 162, 163 bottom, 165, 167 left, 167 right, 168–169, 173 bottom. **Allen, Anthony/ www.aerialphoto.co.za:** pages 150–151. **Apartheid Museum:** pages 44 top, 44 bottom, 45. **Austen, Neil (AfriPics.com):** page 159. **Bannister, Andrew (IOA):** page 32 right. **Beath, Karl (IOA):** pages 78, 154. **Colour Library (IOA):** page 123 bottom. **De la Harpe, Roger (AfriPics.com):** pages 121, 158. **De la Harpe, Roger (IOA):** page 94. **Dennis, Nigel (IOA):** pages 8–9, 22–23, 30–31, 32 top left, 32 centre, 32 bottom left, 33, 36, 54–55, 59, 60–61, 62, 63, 70–71, 76–77, 81 centre, 81 right, 81 bottom, 114–115, 128–129, 138 bottom left, 139, 140, 141, 142, 143, 163 top, 164 left, 164 right. **Dreyer, Gerhard (IOA):** pages 116–117, 120. **Froneman, Albert (IOA):** page 118. **Gallo Images:** pages 18 bottom, 122, 133. **Gubb, Louis (Trace Images):** page 15. **Haestier, Rod (IOA):** page 170. **Harvey, Martin (IOA):** pages 34–35. **Hes, Lex (AfriPics. com):** pages 96–97. **Hoffmann, Leonard (IOA):** page 99. **Johannesburg Tourism:** page 41 left. **Jowell, Jeremy (IOA):** pages 152–153. **Knirr, Walter (AfriPics.com):** pages 38–39. **Knirr, Walter (IOA):** front cover, back cover, pages 17 right centre, 20–21, 41 right, 47, 50–51, 52, 56, 67, 68–69, 72, 73, 75, 80, 81 top left, 98, 108, 130, 172. **Mala Mala Game Reserve:** page 58. **Marais, Johan (IOA):** pages 138 top left, 138 centre, 138 bottom right. **Middleton, Owen (IOA):** pages 24–25. **Moseley, Steve (IOA):** page 134. **Murray, Jax (IOA):** page 43. **Naude-Moseley, Brent (IOA):** page 135. **Olbrich, Bernie (AfriPics.com):** pages 10–11. **Perry, Phil (IOA):** page 37 top. **Pickford, Peter (IOA):** pages 17 top right, 28 bottom centre, 131, 132. **Pinnock, Peter:** page 110. **Pullen, Charles (images24.co.za/Die Burger):** page 18 top. **Reid, Jonathan (IOA):** pages 92–93, 112 bottom. **Setford, Ross (PictureNET Africa):** pages 18 bottom, 19. **Simeone, Giovanni (Sime/Photo Access):** page 46. **Smith, Stephan (IOA):** half title page, pages 160–161. **Source unknown:** page 14 left, 14 right. **Thiel, Erhardt (IOA):** page 28 top left. **TravelStock44/ www.photolibrary.com:** page 155. **Van Jaarsveld, Rhone (IOA):** page 42. **Van Zandbergen, Ariadne (Africa Imagery):** pages 144–145. **Van Zandbergen, Ariadne (IOA):** page 95 right. **Von Hörsten, Friedrich (IOA):** pages 103, 136–137, 156–157. **Von Hörsten, Hein (IOA):** pages 29, 37 bottom, 40, 48–49, 112 top, 124, 125, 166. **Von Hörsten, Lanz (IOA):** title page, pages 28 top centre, 28 top right, 28 bottom left, 28 bottom right, 57, 64–65, 66, 82–83, 100–101, 126–127, 138 top right, 173 top. **Weaving, Alan (AfriPics.com):** page 113. **Weiss, Chanan (IOA):** pages 12, 106–107. **Woodburn, Andrew (IOA):** page 171. **Young, Keith (IOA):** page 105.